ACTIVE REPLAY!

ROLE-PLAYS FOR ENGLISH AND SOCIAL EDUCATION

MIKE DAVIS
and
TIM LONG

Blackwell Education

To both our families, especially Julie for putting up with us, and to Louise

First published 1989

Published by Basil Blackwell Ltd
108 Cowley Road
Oxford OX4 1JF
England

British Library Cataloguing in Publication Data

Davis, Mike

Active Replay!: role plays and simulations for English and personal social education
1. Great Britain. Secondary schools, Moral and Social education. Teaching methods: Role playing exercises
I. Title.   II. Long, Tim
373′.01′140941

ISBN 0-631-16833-8

Typeset in 12/14pt Sabon by
Wearside Tradespools, Fulwell, Sunderland
Printed in Great Britain by
Dotesios Printers Ltd

CONTENTS

ACKNOWLEDGEMENTS

The materials in this book were developed and trialled over a two year period and there are many people who helped in the process of refining the final product. Among these in particular, we would like to thank:

Third, fourth and fifth year pupils at Everton High School, Blackburn, who were willing participants and whose comments were very useful; the staff of the English Department: Margaret Bagshaw, Janis Livesey, Nazir Patel, Sandra Pledger and particularly Pete Wilson who has provided one of the authors with the benefits of his thinking over a twelve year period. Eileen Burton, Head of Third year and Lynne Masters JP, Senior Tutor, from Everton High School both gave support and advice; Lancashire County Council Probation Service, Blackburn were very helpful in supplying factual information about the complexities of sentencing and parole; St. Martin's College, Lancaster, particularly Hugh Roberts and Alan Pound from the English Department and English PGCE students 1987, and Dave Brunton; PC Andy Wilde, Blackburn Police; Mrs Eileen Potiatynik, Welfare Rights Worker, Mustard Seed House, Blackburn; Margaret Ratcliffe and Helen Clarke, and members of Kaleidoscope Youth and Community Centre, Blackburn and especially Tony Parkinson, the Area Youth Worker, for many opportunities to discuss and experiment and for the best School Leaver Course in Lancashire; Father Lee, Our Lady of Perpetual Succour, Blackburn; UK Immigration Advisory Service, Manchester; British Pregnancy Advisory Service, Manchester; Dr. C. J. Hinds, Consultant Anaesthetist and Director of the Intensive Care Unit, St. Bartholomews Hospital, London; Brian Meginnis, Director of Policy and Information, MENCAP, London all gave invaluable information and advice; Caroline Jackson, Head of English at Carr Hill High School, Kirkham for support; and Cath Laing, St. Bede's High School, Ormskirk who convinced us that everything was OK.

Dot King, a colleague from the English Department at Everton High School, made a number of useful suggestions, including the essay titles for Michelle Tyson, and was also a fast and accurate proof reader.

PREFACE

These materials were written in the first instance with GCSE in mind, and Chapter 1 discusses in detail the relationship between role-play and the GCSE National Criteria for English. The publication in June, 1989 of *English for ages 5 to 16: Proposals of the Secretary of State for Education and Science and the Secretary of State for Wales* (hereafter called Cox) has broadened the area of debate. What Cox does is more firmly endorse the beneficial relationship between talk and language development, which is the focus of this book. As Cox says:

> ... talk is now widely recognised as promoting and embodying a range of skills and competence – both transactional and social – that are central to children's overall language development. (15.4)

Cox argues that the growth of oracy is central to language development, and that fluency in spoken language enables pupils to take a full part in the adult community. For example he states:

> As consumers, (pupils) will need to know how to conduct oral transactions effectively – how to seek information, how to negotiate, how to complain. As potential jurors or witnesses, voters or representatives of political or interest groups they will need to know how to judge or present a spoken case, how to recognise emotive language and arguments that are specious or selective, and how to martial facts with clarity and precision. (15.7)

These materials allow for just such language experience. In each role-play pupils are expected to put forward a recommendation based on conflicting evidence, and roles include an MP, Councillors, representatives of pressure groups and a variety of professional people as well as those which give pupils opportunities to take roles that are closer to their own experiences and age.

Cox outlines a set of oral skills by which pupils could demonstrate their growing competence as speakers and listeners:

- developing increasing clarity and precision in describing experience and expressing opinions, and sensitivity in articulating personal feelings;
- formulating – and making appropriate responses to – increasingly complex instructions and questions;
- developing an increasing capacity to organise or sequence information and response;
- demonstrating an increasing ability to evaluate and to reflect;

- incr asingly adjusting language and delivery to suit audience and purpose, and being able – as an audience for others – to understand, respond to and reflect on correspondingly wider modes of address;
- showing an increasing ability to function collaboratively – eg involving others in a discussion; listening to and giving weight to the opinions of others; perceiving the relevance of contributions; timing contributions; adjusting and adapting in feedback;
- showing an increasing ability to be explicit about how written and spoken language can support each other. (15.16)

Cox links these to one specific attainment target:

> The development of pupils' understanding of the spoken word and the capacity to express themselves effectively in a variety of speaking and listening activities, matching style and response to audience and purpose. (15.18)

Role-play is an ideal vehicle for the development of such language performance giving, as it does, the opportunity to develop a range of linguistic skills, both spoken and written. It also provides a vehicle for pupils to develop an understanding of complex issues. As Cox says,

> We see role-play as a valuable means of broadening pupils' mental and emotional horizons and of developing social and personal confidence: it provides an ideal medium for much of the exploratory and/or performance-based elements of programmes of study. (15.23)

Cox identifies specific levels of performance within the Attainment Target for Speaking and Listening. The likely target for the median 16 year old is the boundary between level 6 and 7. The descriptions of performance at level 7 expects a pupil to be able to:

> 7(i) express a point of view cogently and with clarity to a range of audiences and interpret with accuracy a range of statements by others.
>
> 7(ii) understand and use transactional language effectively on occasions where a situation or topic requires more than one outcome and is less readily familiar to the pupils and/or their audience.
>
> 7(iii) take an active part in group discussions, contributing constructively to the development of the argument in hand.

These role-plays will create an environment where this can take place and furthermore will also allow pupils, as part of a post-experience discussion to:

> 7(iv) talk about appropriateness in the use of spoken language, according to purpose, topic and audience.

Each role-play provides ample opportunity for assessment and self-assessment – a feature specifically identified in levels 9 and 10:

> 9(ii) Take an active part in group discussions, displaying sensitivity, listening critically eg to attempts to persuade and being self-critical.

The self-assessment pro forma provided on page 8 will enable pupils to keep a record of their developing competence as they gain experience. In addition to acquiring a record of their linguistic performance, pupils will also develop the techniques of introspection and self-evaluation which are pre-requisites for attaining the highest levels of competence. This process is explored in more detail in *5 Introducing role-play*.

As we discuss *1 Role-play in the English classroom*, we see a close relationship between talk and writing, and the role plays provide a stimulating and 'realistic' context within which pupils can develop their ideas about complex issues. As Cox says:

> Much writing in English will be attempts by pupils to record their thoughts on topics of personal or public importance. Through discussion or role play, teachers should seek to provide frequent opportunities for this type of writing to occur, and should respond to the meanings that their pupils strive to convey. (17.19)

This is achieved through a variety of writing activities from taking notes to more polished pieces of writing (including collection and shaping of information gained in role play) for GCSE course work submissions. The written activities included in these materials aim to promote this.

Further insights into the successful implementation of Spoken English can be gained from the DES Document, *Good Work in English: a survey of good practice in Years 1 to 5 of Secondary Schools* (Report by HMI, 1989) which says that while talk is an excellent vehicle for language development, it can have limitations. HMI says that

> ... wider inspection evidence in English suggests that where an oral lesson is closely focussed upon the improvement or assessment of oral work itself, it often collapses for want of a more identifiably real purpose.

The clear message is that both subject matter and organisation are the keys to the success of good oral work. These role plays perform both functions by presenting a clearly structured set of activities which are of intrinsic interest to pupils.

The primary aim of this collection is to create spoken English activities which actively involve and engage whole classes or larger groups. The activities are developed in the context of issue-based subject matter (the topic of the role-play). We have tried in each case to present the issues within the context of plausible characters and realistic, contemporary scenarios. While some of these are highly contentious, as in the treatment of mentally-handicapped people (Michelle Tyson) or abortion (Cheryl Wilson) we nevertheless feel that they are of concern and interest to young people and demand open consideration. Also, though some of these role-plays are based on actual events, their re-workings are entirely fictitious. We appreciate that role play techniques require some familiarity on the part of both teachers and pupils. Consequently, we have included a set of introductory role-plays which complement content, structure and skills of the main body of materials. Although written with GCSE English in mind, the techniques used, and in some cases the subject matter, are applicable to other subject areas in schools, and to other training environments.

Mike Davis
Tim Long
July 1989

References

English for ages 5 to 16, Department of Education and Science, 1989. Dd 8171904
Good work in English, Department of Education and Science, 1989. INS 56 112/302 160/89 NS 71/87

1 ROLE-PLAY IN THE ENGLISH CLASSROOM

The aims of the GCSE English course include the following:

1.1 1–4   The subject English is to be regarded as a single unified course . . . The course should seek to develop the ability of students to:

1 communicate accurately, appropriately and effectively in speech and writing;
2 understand and respond imaginatively to what they hear, read and experience in a variety of media;
3 enjoy and appreciate the reading of literature;
4 understand themselves and others.

2.1 1–8   The Assessment Objectives . . . must provide opportunities for candidates to demonstrate their ability to:

1 understand and convey information;
2 understand, order and present facts, ideas and opinions;
3 evaluate information in reading material and in other media, and select what is relevant to specific purposes;
4 articulate experience and express what is felt and what is imagined;
5 recognise implicit meaning and attitudes;
6 show a sense of audience and an awareness of style in both formal and informal situations;
7 exercise control of appropriate grammatical structures, conventions of paragraphing, sentence structure, punctuation and spelling in their writing;
8 communicate effectively and appropriately in Spoken English.

The skills listed above are clearly interrelated and interdependent and, whilst all must be assessed, it is not envisaged that each skill need be separately tested.
(GCSE National Criteria Department of Education and Science)

These aims and objectives recognise the danger that the twin demands of integration and the fulfilment of different criteria may come into conflict. This becomes apparent in an approach where too much emphasis is placed on meeting individual criteria, for example, tone of voice. Concentration on individual discrete elements assumes that they can be developed separately from other elements and that there can be a transfer from the isolated practice to the integrated speech situation.

As the GCSE National Criteria continues:

> The use of language represents a variety of combinations of linguistic skills and modes of language. It is not intended that the objectives should be assessed in isolation ... (4.1 Relationship between Assessment Objectives and Content)

It is our belief that any attempt to assess in isolation fails both to fulfil the spirit of GCSE and also fails to maximise the potential of Spoken English as an holistic experience. And what is meant by an holistic experience? Effective Spoken English demands a variety of talking and listening skills from the user. In order to meet such a variety of skills, the English teacher does not need to isolate individual features. To teach discrete skills does not imply that those skills need to be tackled individually. In fact, these skills are only developed within the context of other skills, to develop one skill, the teacher is necessarily drawing upon other skills. For example, in developing tone of voice, the teacher will inevitably draw upon pupils' ability to recognise register (the form of language used in certain circumstances), appropriateness, and audience. Since each discrete skill depends upon other skills, we feel it inappropriate to assess these separately. The materials that we have produced are concerned with individual skills but they are not isolated from the other skills which contribute to performance in the spoken language.

The Northern Examining Association English Syllabus B 1990 *Instructions and guidance for teachers in the internal assessment of Oral Communication* says:

> In a programme of English work pupils are likely to attempt a wide variety of tasks with equally varied demands on their oral ability. At times their work will be directed towards producing a performance, such as:
>
> - a talk
> - a reading
> - a role play
> - a report
> - an interview
> - a narration of an anecdote
> - an explanation
>
> These may be described as *products* as this distinguishes these occasions from situations where oral work occurs in the context of other activities. This *process* work might include
>
> - exploring a poem or story
> - discussing a topic

- preparing a list of questions
- brainstorming
- preparing a statement of findings
- solving a problem (simulation)
- interviewing

On these occasions the eventual product may be oral or written, but since oral work has made a significant contribution to the process it is essential that assessment of oral communication should take account of such occasions. Assessment should include candidates' oral contributions to group work, in the organisation and direction of the activity as well as its content and purpose.

The essential feature of the materials in this collection is that they allow for this variety of Spoken Language skills to be practised and assessed within the one format. Furthermore, just as individual Spoken Language skills need not be practised in isolation, Spoken Language itself need not be isolated from other language activities such as reading and writing.

Although the emphasis of this material is upon the oral component of GCSE English, it provides valuable stimulus for written work and for further reading.

Written English

The GCSE English syllabus recognises the value that Spoken English has in developing language skills in general. These materials lead naturally into written work based very firmly on real experiences as well as meeting the criteria of GCSE written work. Thus the *Michelle Tyson* role-play (see pages 97 to 108) can allow written explorations of the issues discussed through these sample tasks:

1 A conference is to take place to discuss the case of Michelle Tyson. Those present will be:

Miss Charlotte Smith, Director of the Council Home;
Father Frank McGee, Parish Priest;
Dr Sara Foster, Action for Mentally Handicapped representative;
and Ms Farida Patel, representative of Civil Rights Movement

Imagine the conference. Present the views of each person present. If you like you can set your essay down like a play, but remember to indicate the feelings of the speakers.

2 Mr and Mrs Tyson have been asked to take part in a TV programme about the problems of bringing up a mentally handicap-

ped child. Think carefully about the sort of questions they might be asked and about how each one would respond. Remember that Mr and Mrs Tyson will have experienced the problems differently. Write the interview.

3 Write an essay which clearly describes all of the issues that are involved in the case of Michelle Tyson. Next sum up all of the possible solutions. If the decision was yours, how would you treat Michelle? Remember you have to try to find a solution that is best for everyone. You may have to disregard the views of one or more of those involved. Whose views would you disregard? Why? Describe how you came to your decision regarding the case of Michelle Tyson and why you think that yours is the best course of action.

Such essay titles provide the opportunity to develop certain types of writing style which relate directly to a number of criteria for GCSE written assignments. For example:

> Opportunities must be provided to develop a variety of style of writing in what may be termed 'closed' situations (eg the writing of letters, reports and instructions) where the subject matter, form, audience and purpose are largely 'given' and in what may be termed 'open' situations (eg narrative writing, and imaginative/personal response to a range of stimuli and experience) where such factors are largely determined by the writer. (3.3)

6.4 1–7 More specifically, Grade C candidates are expected to demonstrate competence in:

1 understanding and conveying information both at a straightforward and a more complex level;
2 understanding facts, ideas and opinion, and ordering and presenting them with a degree of clarity and accuracy;
3 evaluating materials and selecting what is relevant for specific purposes;
4 describing and reflecting upon experience and expressing effectively what is felt and what is imagined;
5 recognising the more obvious implicit meanings and attitudes;
6 showing a sense of audience and an awareness of uses of language appropriate in different situations;
7 writing in paragraphs using sentences of varied kinds and exercising care over punctuation and spelling.

The suggested written assignments which follow each role play aim to provide an opportunity to develop these writing styles and as such, are consistent with the criteria of GCSE English.

Assessment strategies

During each role-play, we have identified pupils as being involved in one or more of the following activities:

- performing a given role (in the case of the characters);
- performing a formal role (in reporting back);
- setting up and testing hypotheses (during the formulation of questions);
- asking questions (during the interviews);
- responding to questions (during the interviews);
- recognising the appropriate use of language (during interviews);
- communicating facts, ideas, emotions and opinions (during the interviews, in discussion and in report-back);
- sharing interim and final conclusions (during discussion);
- evaluating perceptions of events (during discussion);
- reaching agreement or justifying minority views (during discussion);
- making decisions about the appropriate use of language (during preparation for role-play);
- using imagination to develop roles (during preparation for role-play)
- discovering the complexities of argument (during interviews, discussion and preparation for role-play);
- contextualising abstract ideas (during discussion and preparation for role-play);
- developing abstractions from concrete experiences (during discussion and preparation for role-play);
- acquiring knowledge about specific issues (during discussion and preparation for role-play)

It is the teacher's role to identify which of the above criteria are to be assessed. The method of assessment will inevitably vary, depending on the school and the Examination Board. Each Board has recommended its own method of recording assessment and clearly it is up to the individual school to choose and to develop these accordingly. The sample assessment sheets, see pages 6, 7 and 8 have been found to be useful instruments for making teacher assessments and allowing space for the pupil to record comments about performance. These self-assessment opportunities have been particularly useful in identifying successes and areas for future development.

Candidate's Name

<u>English Group</u>

Spoken English Assessment

This matrix is to be completed with close reference to the Assessment Criteria to be found in the relevant section of the English Syllabus.

Assessment focus / Activity				
WHAT: organised				
relevant				
imaginative				
developed				

HOW: register vocabulary idiom	intonation pace tone	gesture	responsiveness to others	other

Spoken English Self Evaluation Sheet

Name _____   English Group _____

What part did you play in the role play?   In what way(s) do you think you were
_____   successful in the activity?

What do you think you learned from   _____
the activity?

_____   _____

_____   _____

_____   _____

_____   If you were to do a similar assignment in
          the future, what do you feel you would
_____   like to improve?

_____   _____

_____   _____

_____   _____

_____   _____

_____   _____

If the teacher decided to assess the ability to:

- perform a role;
- respond to questions;
- communicate facts, ideas, emotions and opinions;
- make decisions about the appropriate use of language;
- recognise the appropriate use of language;
- use imagination to develop roles;
- acquire knowledge about specific issues,

s/he should concentrate on the role player(s) who will need to display such skills. If, on the other hand, the teacher wishes to assess

- setting up and testing hypotheses;
- asking questions;
- sharing interim and final conclusions;
- reaching agreement or justifying minority views;
- evaluating perceptions of events;
- discovering the complexities of argument;
- contextualising abstract ideas;
- developing abstractions from concrete experiences;
- acquiring knowledge about specific issues,

s/he could look at the performance of pupils in the groups.

In practical terms it is possible for a teacher to vary this and to evaluate between six and ten pupils during a role-play. This can be done in a variety of ways, including:

remaining in one group, and seeing six role-players and between four and six interviewers;
following an individual role-player, and seeing that role-player and many pupils acting as interviewers;
following two role-players, and etc.

The combinations available allow for maximum opportunities to conduct assessments, while at the same time, enabling the remainder of the class to be actively involved in valuable work.

2 RUNNING ROLE-PLAY

On the assumption that the teacher is faced with a class of 25 to 30 pupils, with a lesson lasting no longer than one hour, this is the technique to employ:

1 Desks and chairs need to be arranged to allow for group work.

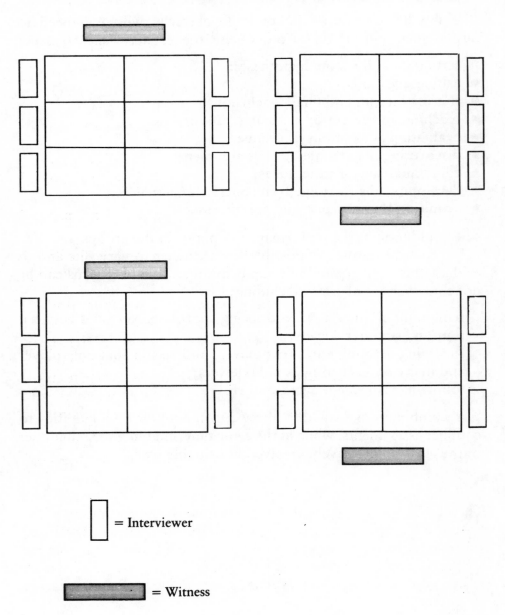

⬜ = Interviewer

▭ = Witness

2 The topic is introduced and then each member of the class is given the Background Information Sheet and is allowed time to read and digest it.

3 The teacher conducts a brief discussion about the information given in the Background Sheet to ensure that all pupils understand the issues. Additional notes that relate to a particular role-play can also be distributed.

4 Pupils are identified to fill each of the roles, and are given a copy of their role sheet. They should be separated from the rest of the class and be given time to read and assimilate their roles. The teacher must be satisfied that the role players have grasped the important elements of their characters. It may be helpful for the role players to read out their role sheets to each other. A short question and answer session will help clarify the roles they are to play. The Role-Play Biography pro forma found on page 12 may be useful.

5 Whilst the role players are preparing, the remainder of the class are divided into groups and are told to formulate questions for each of the characters in role. Each group, consisting of between four and six pupils, should appoint a secretary who should take note of anything that the group considers to be particularly important. The pro forma on page 13 may help to structure the questions and answers.

6 When the teacher is satisfied that the role players and the groups are ready, the role players can be individually introduced into the groups. Each group is allowed five minutes to interview each role player and then the role players change groups. Thus after 30 minutes, each group has interviewed each role player.

7 The groups should then spend up to ten minutes discussing the evidence that they have heard, reaching a conclusion and identifying the justifications for the decision that they have made. While this is taking place, the role players can share their experiences and attempt to come to some agreement as to the likely outcomes of the other groups' deliberations.

These could take the form of free ranging discussions but some teachers may prefer a more structured analysis of the options. One approach suggested by Steve Parr, Curriculum Development Officer with the Economic and Industrial Awareness Programme at Manchester University, is to conduct a Cost/Benefit Analysis. This is an approach which encourages pupils to consider all of the possible advantages and disadvantages of a particular course of action. A sample analysis of some of the costs and benefits of placing

Role Play Biography of _____

Summary of Given Information: _____

_____

_____

_____

_____

_____

Relevant Information from other roles: _____

_____

_____

_____

_____

Further Information developed from above: _____

_____

_____

_____

_____

_____

_____

_____

_____

Title of Role Play

Character _____

Questions	Responses

Group View:

_____

_____

_____

_____

_____

Jonathan Banks in Youth Custody is shown on page 15. The approach also encourages the following questions:

- what do we hope to achieve by making this decision?
- does our decision represent the 'best' use of resources?
- will the outcomes of our decision be in the 'best' interests of all sections of society or just some?
- what are the costs and benefits of our decision? (money/non-money, private/social including environmental impact)
- what alternative decisions could we have taken?
- how would these affect society and individuals? (further cost and benefit analysis)
- what constraints exist to limit or influence our choice? (social, political, cultural and moral factors)
- do values and actions always correspond?

Clearly, this approach is not going to be possible in the short period of time at the end of the role-play but it could form the basis for follow up activities, both oral and written.

8 The class can now return to a plenary session and each group should present its conclusions and justifications and raise any other issues related to the role-play.

These timings are approximate and individual teachers will be able to adjust them to suit local circumstances. For example, if lessons are less than an hour, part of a first session could be spent looking at the Background Sheet; a second complete session could be used to conduct the interviews; and a third session could allow for group discussion and report back. Alternatively, teachers may wish to identify four characters to be interviewed and introduce the views of the remainder by distributing copies of the remaining role sheets.

Clearly teachers may develop other ways of using these materials to suit their own needs and those of their pupils.

The flow chart on pages 16 and 17 illustrates the process and draws attention to the Assessment Objectives at each stage of the activity.

A sample Cost/Benefit Analysis

In the event of Jonathan Banks being sent for a period of Youth Custody

Money Costs	Money Benefits
Personal: Loss of family allowance; loss of income after leaving school; cost of visiting.	Personal: Not having to pay for upkeep.
Social: £x per week paid by taxpayer through The Home Office.	Social: Local Authority saves cost of education; Department of Social Security saves Family Allowance; Youth Custody cheaper than Residential Schooling.
Non-Money Costs	**Non-Money Benefits**
Personal: Likelihood of re-offending; closer association with criminal sub-culture; family reputation (particularly younger boys).	Personal: Less trouble in the family home; no worries about further criminal behaviour.
Social: Loss of freedom; loss of contact with family; loss of educational opportunities.	Social: School loses troublesome pupil; society protected from criminal behaviour.

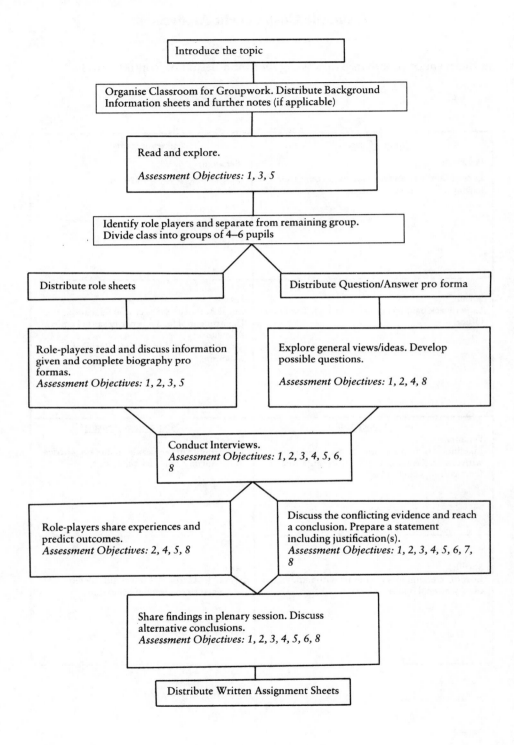

Introduce the topic

Organise Classroom for Groupwork. Distribute Background Information sheets and further notes (if applicable)

Read and explore.

Assessment Objectives: 1, 3, 5

Identify role players and separate from remaining group. Divide class into groups of 4–6 pupils

Distribute role sheets

Distribute Question/Answer pro forma

Role-players read and discuss information given and complete biography pro formas.
Assessment Objectives: 1, 2, 3, 5

Explore general views/ideas. Develop possible questions.

Assessment Objectives: 1, 2, 4, 8

Conduct Interviews.
Assessment Objectives: 1, 2, 3, 4, 5, 6, 8

Role-players share experiences and predict outcomes.
Assessment Objectives: 2, 4, 5, 8

Discuss the conflicting evidence and reach a conclusion. Prepare a statement including justification(s).
Assessment Objectives: 1, 2, 3, 4, 5, 6, 7, 8

Share findings in plenary session. Discuss alternative conclusions.
Assessment Objectives: 1, 2, 3, 4, 5, 6, 8

Distribute Written Assignment Sheets

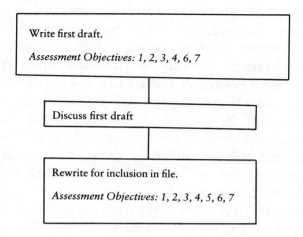

This flow chart refers to the following GCSE Assessment Objectives:

1 understand and convey information;
2 understand, order and present facts, ideas and opinions;
3 evaluate information in reading material and in other media, and select what is relevant to specific purposes;
4 articulate experience and express what is felt and what is imagined;
5 recognise implicit meaning and attitudes;
6 show a sense of audience and an awareness of style in both formal and informal situations;
7 exercise control of appropriate grammatical structures, conventions of paragraphing, sentence structure, punctuation and spelling in their writing;
8 communicate effectively and appropriately in Spoken English.

The role plays that follow are very different from the more traditional type that simply provide biographical data where attitudes, personality and perception have to be assumed with little or no assistance from the information itself. The successful realisation of these role characters can only be achieved when attitude and perception become a dominant feature of the role players' performances. Though factual information is of importance, it is subsumed by the personality of the role which, experience has shown, arises naturally from the role descriptions whatever format these take. The ability to play the roles successfully does not depend on acting ability but on the ability to identify with the attitudes and perceptions of the characters described.

In early drafts, all of the role plays were presented as simple third person descriptions and these worked very well. We subsequently experimented with different formats for presenting the role play material. This was done for two reasons, first for variety and second, to give the opportunity to present materials as a reading exercise, thereby reducing the number of role players. The materials in this format (report, letter, dialogue etc) can, however, still be used as a basis for role play and in our experience, no problems have been encountered. In some cases third person descriptions are given alongside documentation in other formats. Teachers can choose whether to use either one or both of these.

3 SOME OUTCOMES

Michelle Tyson was chosen as an ideal case study for a formal assessment at the end of the fourth year for all pupils following the GCSE English course. It would allow staff to conduct some assessments of Oral Communication and provide a useful stimulus for the type of writing that many young people find the most difficult, that is, the exploration of complex ideas in an appropriate register.

On a sunny afternoon in June, ninety-four 15 year old pupils gathered in the hall where the examination desks were set out for end-of-year examinations and it was explained to them that they were to begin a four-part process: a) that they would take part in a role play; b) that they would be given a list of written assignments at the end of the afternoon and that they had one week to research, make notes, discuss with staff and pupils and write a draft; c) that on the following Tuesday, under examination conditions, they would write their essays and hand them in with all notes; and d) they would have the opportunity to redraft in the light of the comments made by teachers.

The year was then divided into two halves, each with two members of staff. One group was sent to the Library and one to the fourth form centre. The Background Information sheets were distributed and briefly discussed in plenary and then seven pupils were identified as role players. These seven were told to read their role sheets and to discuss them. The remainder of the group, numbering 40 pupils were divided randomly into four groups of seven and two groups of six. They were asked to re-read the Background Information sheets and then to begin to discuss the issues and explore each others' views in advance of hearing the witnesses. The role players, in the meantime, explored their characters, seeking clarification and help from each other and from one of the teachers.

The activity lasted for over two hours and produced some interesting comments about the structure:

> It helped me to sort out information easily and to make up my own mind and prepare my views to be put on paper the following week. (Ifzal)

Ifzal went on to say:

> I think I learnt to analyse information and people's feelings in greater depth and perception. It's easier to ask questions in a group as long as they all take part with enthusiasm. I find the notes taken during the role-play were extremely helpful during the essay for reference to the people's (role-players') answers, feelings and ideas on the subject.

Not all pupils revealed the same depth of understanding of their own learning processes but most grasped the complexities of the arguments presented by the role-players and recognised the very real dilemma presented by 'real life' cases like Michelle Tyson. Carl, a member of an interviewing group, was able to develop the appropriate register for his TV interview:

> *Miss Smith:* Well personally I think that Michelle should be sterilized to prevent her getting pregnant and causing distress to her and her family.
>
> *Father McGee:* But what gives you the right to prevent a life? What authority says you can stop just who you want from getting pregnant just because you think it would be a strain on the council home?
>
> *Miss Smith:* I am not saying it would not be an added strain on the home but you have to take into account the strain it would be on Michelle giving birth to a child she could never keep. And the strain on Michelle's family if they chose to look after the child who would most likely be handicapped itself.
>
> *Dr Foster:* I also agree with Miss Smith by saying sterilizing would be one method but not the one I would put first . . .
>
> *Father McGee:* But what if Michelle made a recovery and decided she wanted to start a family, what would you say? 'Oh, sorry, we sterilized you.' I think that would be a major upset to her.
>
> *Miss Smith:* I must say that the chance of recovery are almost zero.
>
> *Father McGee:* Yes, you said almost and as long as there is a shred of doubt I say that Michelle Tyson should not undergo any form of treatment to prevent her giving birth to a new life and should not be denied that feeling of life inside her. That feeling that every woman in the world has when giving birth.
>
> *Dr Foster:* If I would be allowed for just one moment, I

would like to get across my views. Although I agree with Miss Smith I could put a better method forward. A way of preventing Michelle getting pregnant without, in future if she was to recover due to some sort of new drug or treatment, denying her the right to start a family.
Father McGee: Which is . . .
Dr Foster: The supervised use of some form of mechanical or chemical contraceptive.
Father McGee: You mean pumping her full of drugs? No. I protest most strongly.

as was Harjinder, another interviewer:

Interviewer: When you found out that your daughter was mentally handicapped how did you feel? If we could come to you first, Mr Tyson.
Mr Tyson: Well naturally we were astonished and very hurt. Not only because she was mentally handicapped but because she's our only child and we wanted to do everything right for her, which we cannot do now.
Interviewer: Mrs Tyson, how did you respond when you heard she was mentally handicapped?
Mrs Tyson: Well at first I couldn't believe it and when it finally did get through to me I just didn't know what to do.
Interviewer: You just said you didn't know what to do. Does this mean you didn't try to cope with her?
Mr Tyson: Well of course we tried to cope with her. Which mother and father wouldn't? We tried everything but in the end it was too much.
Interviewer: When you say too much, in what way was it?
Mr Tyson: Well, she was an increasingly intolerable strain. But on the other hand she could also do things normally.

Despite the difference between mental handicap and mental illness being explained to them, most pupils still took an optimistic view of future medical breakthrough in the treatment of handicap. Virtually all pupils identified closely with the difficulties presented by the case and although sterilization was the most commonly suggested solution, there was understanding of and empathy with all the characters involved.

This was also true when the same group tackled the thorny issue of abortion. *Cheryl Wilson* deals with the dilemma faced by a girl who wants an abortion in the face of opposition from her parents. Cindy, who played Karen Burton, the Childcare teacher, had to deal with the problem of not agreeing with her role. In fact she was vehement in her opposition to abortion. Her written work is a description of the conversation between Cheryl and Karen Burton when she first tells her she is pregnant. Cindy's first draft was read out to one of the authors and the discussion about the work was transcribed:

MD: Right.

CT: It's different.

MD: You started to say what . . . tell me what you were doing.

CT: Well, I tried to do a different sort of writing – something I haven't done before. I knew what I wanted to put down but I just . . . it was just that I couldn't put myself into a position I hadn't been in before and it turned out all wrong.

MD: Tell me what it was that you tried to do.

CT: I was trying to put myself in the position of either a teacher being told about a child that's pregnant or a child trying to tell the teacher and it didn't work either way.

MD: Why didn't it work?

CT: I don't know. I just couldn't get it down right.

MD: So you felt that the language that you were using didn't sound like sort of natural language that people use when they are talking to each other.

CT: It just didn't sound the sort of things they'd say.

MD: Can you read a bit to me?

CT: 'Cheryl Wilson. Conversation between Cheryl and her Childcare teacher Karen Burton when she tells her she is pregnant. It is a Tuesday Afternoon and school has just finished. Cheryl Wilson has just arrived to see Karen Burton about a problem she has got. Cheryl: Miss I need to talk to you about something . . . it's really important.'

MD: Right, hang on a minute. Let's track back a little bit because I know we're recording here but think as well as that . . . to develop the story. Do you think that the girl would jump in immediately with that sort of statement or is she likely to try and find a way around it?

CT: She's sort of trying to find a way around it, around

saying it, but that's where I'm lost. I can't do it as somebody that age would.

MD: You've identified it as a problem but it's not real enough. Anyway, keep going.

CT: 'Karen: Come and sit down and just take your time Cheryl. Now tell me exactly what it is that's bothering you and try not to leave anything important out.

Cheryl: (beginning to cry) For quite a while now I have been sleeping with my boyfriend, John and now I am pregnant but I don't want a baby especially at my age.

Karen: (looking rather disappointed) Cheryl this is something I would never have expected from you but there is no point in lecturing you because what is done is done and all we can do is help you to make sure that you make the right decision as it will affect you for the rest of your life.'

MD: That's OK...

CT: I understand up to a point what I'm doing. It's just the first bit I've got totally wrong. That's where I've got lost in it. I know myself that I've done wrong but it's just trying to correct it that's making it difficult.

MD: Keep going.

CT: 'Cheryl: I have made a decision and told my parents that I want an abortion but they won't agree to it. They are trying to force me into having the child that I just don't want and would never be able to love.

Karen: If you are absolutely sure that this is what you want, I will see if there is anything I can do to help you.

Cheryl: I decided that I wanted an abortion and John is willing to stand by me whatever my decisions are.

Karen: From what you have told me it is hard to understand exactly how you are feeling so your decision is going to have deep emotional effects on you for the rest of your life so you need to be absolutely sure of what you are going to do for the rest of your life before you decide to go ahead with an abortion. I think I understand how most teenagers think so whatever you do don't have an abortion by thinking it will be the easiest way out and will end all your problems because it won't, it just might make everything seem worse.

Cheryl: I am not having an abortion to try and solve any problem, I want an abortion because I don't want an unloved child brought into the world. My parents are not giving me any kind of support at all. They are forcing me to have the child that I don't want. It is them that want the child not me but they don't seem to understand how I feel about all this. After everything that has happened I have got to be grateful to them because they are not blaming everything on John and I am still allowed to see him because they would rather know what I am doing and who I am with than have me lying to them.

Karen: There is not much I can really do to help you apart from maybe having a talk with your parents for you which may not do any good but you don't know until you try. I could also be here whenever you need a sympathetic ear, so go back home and have another talk with your parents and then come back to me and let me know what happens, all right?

Cheryl: Thank you very much for listening to me. It has made me feel a lot better just talking to someone who cares about how I actually feel.'

MD: Right. Just listening to it that once I think I can identify what it is that you've done and you're using quite a formal ... I'll tell you what it sounds like, somebody writing very formal English as if the young person and the teacher are both making speeches to each other rather than having a conversation ...

CT: So that's where I'm lost. It's 'cos I've been trying to put myself in that position but I don't know about anybody who's been in that position so I can't really talk to them to find out how they dealt with it themselves.

MD: Yes.

CT: Something like that would probably help a bit.

MD: I don't think that's so much the problem. I think you've got enough imagination to work it out. I mean all you've got to do is put yourself in the place of Cheryl. I know it's a leap and I know what your views are but take that few steps away from yourself and say, well 'What would I feel like?' and I think that you'll get that without difficulty. I think the harder task will be to try and get the words that people actually say when they're speaking to each other. You know, that slightly more informal ...

CT: I understand the sort of things they say because when I did those diaries I'd a mixture of all different kinds of speaking. I enjoyed doing that. It were easier to come once I got going. It's just that first bit. Once I got the first bit done it all comes easy.

MD: I don't want you to spend too long on the red herring tale, you know, just *I'm really fed up miss*, that sort of conversation. Make it a teacher if you want and leave the teacher a bit of space: *What is it love? Well, I don't know how to tell you. Come on, you know I'm prepared to listen*. That sort of thing. It's the sort of thing that oils the machinery of the conversation. And perhaps the other mistake that you've made is that the speeches that you've got the teacher and the girl making are a little bit long. I think it would be that the girl would hesitate, the teacher would make a comment *Oh I know that's the right thing*. You know it'd be that sort of interjection. And what we're looking for is that sort of natural language of people speaking. It's a very difficult form to write, I mean it really is quite hard to write. But we do interrupt each other and we do say 'yeh', 'um, um' and we do overtalk [*Um, I know what you mean*] each other and all those sorts of things and I think you'll get it right. And I think the message, the actual content of what you are saying is right, it reflects exactly the discussion and the debate that went on in the role-play on Friday. But it's just down to you identifying the right sort of language that people use.

CT: I think I understand now what I have to do. I'll have another go at it, see what comes of it. I'm fed up of doing the same sort of things that's why I did it this way, I wanted to say something different.

MD: I think it's a good first effort and I'm appreciative of the fact that you've identified it as a problem rather than something that you just dash off and say, *Well look – this is what would happen*. You could hand that in and we would say, *Yeh, you've identified the argument, you've identified the fact that this person had those views and this person had those views* but what we're looking for is you identifying the sort of speech and the sort of language that people use in those circumstances. And it's much less formal and much more hesitant and there's much more your turn, my turn rather than like at the moment I'm talking a lot and you're listening and that's OK because it's a different sort of setting but in the sort of thing I'm talking about, you'd have pauses, you'd have well *anything else* or you know all sorts of those little things that help people to carry on a conversation. You could afford to be that hesitant. It could be, you know, quite an extended piece of work. I don't want you to murder yourself about it but obviously you've thought about it quite seriously so far and it would be a shame to lose that.

CT: At first I thought I'd forget it and just throw this

away and start all over again and then I realised *Why should I?* If I want to do it like this, I want to try something different then I'm going to have to carry on.

MD: I think what you have to do is actually put that on one side, keep it next to you, and start the conversation again and start it with these hesitations and don't worry about it if it looks disjointed. I mean the girl will be upset, she would perhaps be crying. As I said, the problem is you dive straight in.

Cindy worked on her ideas and brought in the following version:

'It is a Tuesday afternoon and school has just finished. Cheryl Wilson has arrived to see Karen Burton about a problem she has got.

Cheryl: Miss, can I talk to you about something ... it's really important.

Karen: Of course you can talk to me, that's what I'm here for.

Cheryl: Well, (PAUSE) Well it's this problem I've got.

Karen: What problem is this Cheryl? (SILENCE) Come on now Cheryl. You've got this far. You can tell me anything and I'll do what I can to help you, I promise.

Cheryl: Well it's hard to tell you. I don't know how to put it into words.

Karen: Come on, don't be shy. Just tell me in any way you can what it is that's bothering you.

Cheryl: Well Miss, it's this ...

Karen: This what? (PAUSE) I can't help you if you don't tell me what's bothering you, can I?

Cheryl: It's Mr Batey, Miss.

Karen: What about Mr Batey?

Cheryl: He keeps picking on me.

Karen: Is that all? (Cheryl starts crying) I didn't mean it like that, Cheryl. I just thought it was something really awful.

Cheryl: It's just that I find it hard to understand Chemistry and I can't do my homework so he shouts at me all the time.

Karen: I thought you were good at Sciences? (SILENCE) Aren't you? (SILENCE) Is there anything else wrong Cheryl?

Cheryl: Well ...

Karen: Come on. There is something else isn't there?

Cheryl: (starting to cry) I can't tell you, Miss.

Karen: Well if you don't want me to help ...

Cheryl: I didn't say that Miss.

Karen: Tell me then.

Cheryl: You can't help. It's too horrible.

Karen: What makes you think I can't help you?

Cheryl: I just don't think you can help me, Miss.

Karen: Right then, Cheryl. We'll make a deal.

Cheryl: What sort of deal?

Karen: The deal is . . . you tell me what it is that's really bothering you and if it's possible to help you in any way, I'll help. (SILENCE) Well what do you say, Cheryl?

Cheryl: OK, Miss, I'll tell you. (Cheryl starts crying again and between sobs . . .) I'm pregnant, Miss.

Karen: Oh . . .

Cheryl: I suppose like everybody else you think I'm a slag.

Karen: No, Cheryl. I don't think that. It's just that I never expected anything like this to happen to you.

Cheryl: It could have been anyone. I just wish it wasn't me because I don't want a baby yet.

Karen: Do your parents know about it?

Cheryl: Yes, I told them last week.

Karen: What did they say?

Cheryl: They were pretty angry at first but now . . .

Karen: What?

Cheryl: They want me to have the baby, but I don't.

Karen: What then?

Cheryl: I want an abortion.

Karen: Do you have any chance of convincing them that you don't want to have this baby? Will they agree to it?

Cheryl: No, they don't really care how I feel.'

In this second piece, Cindy was able to show her understanding of the issues and also to identify and reproduce the register that was appropriate to the context. She found the writing quite hard at first but considered her second version to be a big improvement on the first.

The written work assignments at the end of each role-play are only intended as possibles. Teachers will be able to identify issues that they want classes to explore and some pupils may well want to respond in very personal terms. It will be up to individual teachers to decide the exact nature of the written outcomes that they need to meet GCSE criteria.

4 ROLE-PLAY IN NON-GCSE ENGLISH SITUATIONS

Although these role-plays were designed with the Secondary English classroom in mind, they have proved to be extremely useful and enjoyable experiences in other settings including Youth Clubs, Nurse, Youth Worker and Teacher Training (both initial and In-Service). Although the techniques are fundamentally the same as in a school, there are some differences in organisational requirements and in outcomes.

It is likely, for instance, in a Youth Club setting that groups would be smaller, of mixed age, and the situation could be more fluid (given the 'voluntary' nature of youth work practice). Space may present different sorts of constraint but there may be more staff available.

Given this range of differences that may exist, the worker would have to be satisfied that certain conditions were possible:

- suitable space is available – enough room for the interviewers and a separate space for the role-players;
- that the space could not be overlooked or overheard – participants would find an audience intimidating;
- that the group enjoyed coherence and mutual support to allow the role-players particularly to develop their roles without fear of ridicule. It may be necessary to spend a number of sessions designed to develop this atmosphere using the usual 'ice-breaker' activities and some of the introductory materials contained in this volume.

In some cases, it may be desirable to make a 'contract' with the young people who are going to take part in a series of activities. This has the effect of getting a greater degree of commitment from those taking part while at the same time excluding others who would not be able to attend each session or those for whom the working style was inappropriate.

The trial experiences of using these materials were extremely enjoyable but different to those in schools. The debrief discussions were more intense because they involved fewer people. On the other hand, there were no written outcomes, the voluntary nature of the Youth Service precludes this. The practical activity has to stand on its own merits as an enjoyable learning experience and one in which young people can explore problems in a safe, structured environment.

Tony Parkinson, an Area Youth Worker in Blackburn, made the following observations after experiencing a number of trial sessions:

> a) young people were given the opportunity to see others' points of view and these points of view were legitimised by having someone support them – this could shake them out of their complacency!
> b) there were a number of unexpected social outcomes that could be explored in further discussion and debrief, for example, the dominance on more than one occasion of girls;
> c) the technique can be used to explore issues that young people bring to the setting;
> d) adults and young people start out equally and the staff cannot act arbitrarily, there is an opportunity to share the learning experience;
> e) the demands made by literacy help the group to be mutually supportive – less able readers, for example, can be helped through the text to gain an understanding of the issues;
> f) they have fun, if they didn't, they wouldn't turn up the following week!

Developing a curriculum for the Youth Service is less straightforward in some respects than for schools. The ultimate sanction possessed by the young people is not to attend. Our experiences at the Kaleidoscope persuade us of the value of this approach.

Michelle Tyson has been used on a number of occasions by Tom Bradley, a Staff Training Officer responsible for Mental Handicap training in South West Durham Health Authority. He has also used it with groups of student nurses. He comments:

> The issues raised by the materials were pertinent to the objective of the exercise, which was to study and debate the subject of sterilization of people with learning difficulties. Having more time than a school and working with a group more sophisticated concerning current issues in mental handicap, the session developed into consideration of areas away from the main theme and into aspects of self-determination, advocacy and basic human rights. Due to the strengths of the roles described, it was also interesting and useful for the group to look at the situation from different perspectives. Seeing the point of the alternative argument, while not producing definite conclusions, was useful in raising awareness of the two sides which developed. All in all, I found using the materials to be extremely relevant in creating a situation where the topic could be openly debated. Some care did have to be taken at the end of the session, as the factions were quite split, so time was needed for people to de-role and bring the group back to a whole.

As in the authors' experiences of using the materials with adults on PGCE and in-service courses, the outcomes here are much more intense. Adults can show a deeper understanding of the issues and are often more accomplished role-players. Because of this, the extent of disagreement is high and participants' recognition of an 'orthodoxy' does not make the dilemma any less intense. In an exercise not included in this volume, a male post-graduate English student lost a night's sleep after playing the role of a man accused of rape. He commented on the intensity of feelings, shown by a largely female interviewing panel that had decided that he had committed the rape but that there was insufficient evidence to institute proceedings. His experience points out the need for a very thorough debrief designed to remind participants of the fictional nature of the exercise. As Gordon, a fourth year pupil once remarked, *'People start believing that the person being interviewed is the real person in the story and start getting angry with them.'* Paula also commented on this feature: *'I think it was getting to the point when people were beginning to get the idea that I really was Cheryl and I was being called cruel for wanting an abortion. I was only playing the character I was given. I wouldn't want an abortion although I could understand what Cheryl felt.'*

It is these social outcomes that are important in the Social Education settings, for while the issues are of interest in the English classroom, they are not paramount – the content being the vehicle for the process.

Janis Livesey, Head of Personal and Social Education at Queen's Park High School, and also an experienced English teacher, identified the following social outcomes of the role-play techniques employed in this collection. They:

- assist in group-building skills;
- develop decision-making skills;
- encourage appropriate questioning techniques;
- encourage assertiveness as opposed to aggression;
- increase self-confidence;
- help in the process of developing and making value judgements;
- encourage tolerance;
- encourage self-confidence and self-worth;
- encourage an awareness of social issues;
- develop empathy;
- do not allow participants to drop out – everyone has the opportunity to contribute. Asking questions in a small group is

much less threatening than expressing an opinion in a large group. Aysha once wrote: '*I think this activity is very good especially for a person like me because I don't talk or argue with anyone. It's given me a bit of confidence. I think I need a lot to do to give me a lot of confidence.*';

- they allow for the introduction of ideas and views that represent a wide spectrum of opinion, the teacher can introduce unpopular ideas and opinions without anyone having to 'own' them;
- they encourage awareness of others;
- they encourage active listening.

George York was used in an INSET programme for Records of Achievement in English to demonstrate the variety of assessment opportunities that structured role-playing could generate. On that occasion, six people role-played to a group of four interviewers in a fish-bowl, the rest of the course observing the interaction between the participants. On this occasion the role-play served a number of functions:

- demonstrating the variety of speech acts that could be assessed — from the most informal (deciding who was to record information) to the most formal (announcing the recommendation of the group);
- providing an exemplary piece of work which combined process and product that could be used in schools (a number of teachers did ask to be allowed to take the material away and try it in their own schools);
- demonstrating the self-assessment techniques that are a prerequisite of records of Achievement.

The non-GCSE English uses of these materials will be determined largely by the needs that groups bring to them. In social and personal education they give opportunities for practice in decision making and asking valuable questions. They can provide a vehicle for the giving of information, encourage empathy and support group work. In working with adult groups they can do all the above while deepening understanding of the conflicting ideas and opinions surrounding each topic.

5 INTRODUCING ROLE-PLAY

The bulk of the materials in this collection require some experience of role-play techniques in both teachers and pupils. Recognising this need, we include a series of activities which can help prepare a class for the more demanding and complex role-plays which follow.

These introductory materials, however, are not a pre-requisite for the successful use of the later materials and individual teachers will be able to decide for themselves which, if any, are appropriate to their classes.

All of the following practice items employ some of the skills and techniques of the later role plays and also imply a flexible classroom environment designed to encourage group work.

Practice Activity 1 *Who Am I?*

Aim

To familiarise pupils with questioning techniques and group work.

Method

1 The teacher should tell the class that s/he is a famous person (for example, John Wayne, Margaret Thatcher) and that the class has to discover his/her assumed identity by asking questions which can only be answered by the words *Yes, No* or *Irrelevant*. For example, *Are you male? Are you alive? Are you English? Are you a politician?* Continue until the identity is correctly identified.
2 Repeat until confident that the class is familiar with the technique.
3 Allow pupils to form small groups and allow each member in turn to assume an identity and be questioned about it in the same way.
4 The assessment focus will be based largely on how successful class members were in identifying the characters. Success would depend on the following features:

   a) asking the right sort of questions;

b) listening to questions and answers – particularly important to avoid repetition;

c) summarising – an occasional recap is necessary to check on what has been discovered.

The teacher will need to debrief the group on these features and on subsequent occasions remind the group of the demands of good questioning.

Practice Activity 2 *Where Were You . . . ?*

Aim

To develop more varied types of questioning and to introduce elements of ambiguity in evidence.

Method

1 The teacher should explain that s/he is going to accuse two pupils of committing an offence at a particular time on a particular day, for example *I believe that you two scratched a car last night at 4.30 on Stanley Street.*
2 The two pupils must then leave the room and establish an alibi. Whilst they are out of the room, the rest of the class are told that their responsibility is to ask a series of questions in order to establish the truth, or otherwise, of the alibi.
3 The accused are then invited one at a time back into the classroom where they are questioned about their whereabouts at the time of the offence. What the class is looking for is any evidence of inconsistency regarding the alibi. The teacher may offer a model of good questions, for example, *Where were you at 4.30 pm on Saturday?*, *Who were you with?*
4 The conclusion is a verdict of guilty or not guilty.
5 This could be repeated in smaller groups.
6 As in the previous practice activity, assessment is made of the quality of the questioning and the ability to listen effectively with the additional need to consider the likelihood of one version of truth over another.

Practice Activity 3 The Second-Hand Car

NB The emphasis of this and the following activities switches from an assessment of factual evidence to one of evaluating opinions and perceptions.

Aim

To introduce simple role play techniques involving shared background information (see page 36) and one role player.

Method

1 The teacher distributes the background sheet and allows time for the pupils to consider questions that they may wish to ask. The question/response pro forma (see page 13) may be used if desired. Pupils may need prompting as to the sort of questions to ask. What they will find, however, is a considerable difference between the evidence of the two sides in the dispute and this in itself generates many spontaneous questions to Mrs Tyde.

2 The teacher or a confident class member enters the following role.

> You are a twenty-nine year old married woman and you have just had a baby so you have been forced to sell your Triumph Spitfire. You had always looked after it very carefully and although not claiming it to be perfect you were quite happy that it was roadworthy, as its MOT showed. You used the car every day and spent a lot of time looking after it.
>
> You saw Mr Wilson driving it on a number of occasions and it was obvious to you that he was an inexperienced driver who, you thought, really drove too quickly.
>
> You are confident that when you sold the car, it was in a good condition and that its present state reflects on Mr Wilson's driving. You resent his accusation that you knowingly sold him a car that claimed to have a recon-ditioned engine and new clutch. It is quite clear that any car that had these improvements would not be selling for the price that you agreed.

3 The pupils are then given the opportunity to question the role player.

4 The class is then divided into groups of four to eight and asked to consider whether they believe Mrs Tyde's version or Mr Wilson's version of events.

5 The whole class can then share their findings together. The conflict between the given written evidence and the spoken evidence of Mrs Tyde will need to be explored. Groups will have to present justifications for supporting one party or the other.

6 Assessment needs to focus on

   a) reading the information carefully

   b) the ability of members of the class to handle the two contradictory versions of events.

To *what extent is the information given orally or in writing 'the truth, the whole truth and nothing but the truth'?* Teachers should point out the different perceptions that people can have of the same event and that people are quite capable of simply hearing what they want to hear and believing what they want to believe. What the pupils are looking for is *'a balance of probabilities'* rather than *'beyond reasonable doubt'* – a subtle but important distinction. One possible outcome may be that pupils give more credibility to the written evidence than the oral evidence. In this case, the teacher should role-play Mr Wilson and portray him in slightly less than favourable light, for example:

Q: Where have you driven the car?
A: Oh, around town, you know. When I've been out with my friends for a drink.
Q: Do you mean that you drink and drive?

It is the complexity and ambiguity of the issue that need to be explored and this may need encouragement.

The second hand car

Background information

Mr Wilson is a twenty-three year old dental assistant who has just passed his driving test and although short of money has bought his first car from Mrs Tyde for £900. He had always wanted a sports car so when he saw the following advertisement, he was very keen to buy.

> TRIUMPH SPITFIRE (1973) L reg. 9 months MOT and tax. Good runner. Used daily. Clean. Radio. Soft top. Various recent new parts. £950 ono. Phone Mrs Tyde 53677.

Mr Wilson phoned Mrs Tyde and went around to see the car. She took him for a trial run and told him that it has just had a reconditioned engine, a new clutch and some welding under the sills.

He managed to persuade Mrs Tyde to accept £900 and he drove home.

The car went well for the first three weeks but then the problems began, minor at first, but eventually after four weeks, the engine siezed up and Mr Wilson had to call in a mechanic. He examined the car and said,

> This wasn't a very wise buy. There isn't a reconditioned engine and the clutch is badly worn. You should have had it checked before you bought it. There are too many people making a killing from innocent punters like you. My advice is 'never buy a second-hand car without having someone check it.'

You now have an opportunity to confront Mrs Tyde with the allegations that she sold a car that was not in the condition she claimed it to be.

The second hand car

Written assignments

1 Write the conversation between Mrs Tyde and Mr Wilson

   a) when he buys the car and
   b) when he first complains to her about it.

2 Write a letter of complaint from Mr Wilson. Write Mrs Tyde's reply.

3 Imagine that you are either Mr Wilson or Mrs Tyde. Rewrite the whole episode from your point of view.

Practice Activity 4 Youth Club Disco

Aim

To introduce simple role play techniques involving shared background information (see page 40) and two role players.

Method

1 The teacher distributes the Background Information sheet and allows time for the pupils to consider questions that they may wish to ask. The question/response pro forma (see page 13) may be used if desired. Pupils may need prompting as to the sort of questions to ask.

2 Either the teacher plus one pupil or two pupils are given the role sheets. Pupils may benefit from using the role-play biography sheet (see page 12).

3 The class is divided into two groups and have an opportunity to interview each of the role players in turn.

4 Having interviewed both characters, each group should reach a conclusion and then should share their ideas in a class discussion. In each case, the groups should justify the decision they have made.

5 As in the case of *The Second-Hand Car*, the assessment focuses on:

   a) how successful pupils were in understanding the given written information;

   b) translating that understanding into successful role-playing;

   c) translating that understanding into appropriate questions;

   d) making judgements about what is read and heard;

   e) persuading others of a point of view.

The assessment at this and other introductory stages should be formative, identifying areas for improvement in future and the possibilities for more complex activities. A teacher may find him/herself saying:

> As a class you managed the exercise quite well. Most of the group asked appropriate questions although some of you did not listen to the answers and repeated questions already asked by others in the group.

The pupil self-assessment sheet generated these comments:

> I think I will have to improve my answering of the questions and not be too scared. (*Manawar, role-player*)

I don't think I performed as well as I could have because I made my mind up before asking any questions or listening to any answers. (*Carol, interviewer*)

I learned to think of an immediate answer to a question. I think my performance was fairly good but I should try to give more elaborate answers. (*David, role-player*)

I need to ask questions that matter and say what I feel, not what others feel. (*Mark, interviewer*)

I got on well. It was enjoyable being a chairperson and deciding things. I made a good effort at it and spoke well English. I like arguing. It's good and fun. (*Safina, interviewer*)

I injoyed not haveing to rite enthing. I larned how to aask qusthons. I thing ther shod be mor qustitons and mor pepolls. (*Anon, interviewer*)

This last example written by a boy with a reading age 7·5 illustrates the suitability of the technique for all pupils. He did, in fact, become a competent questioner and, with assistance, managed a role quite successfully.

Youth club disco

Background information

Sylvie Thomson is a fourteen year old pupil at Hey Lane Comprehensive School where she has just joined the fourth year doing GCSE courses in seven subjects. She is popular at school and has developed a close circle of friends with whom she spends most of her time both in and out of school.

During the summer holidays she helped out at a summer play scheme for younger children and enjoyed it so much that she is considering the idea of working with children in some capacity when she leaves school.

She has a good relationship with her parents, and although not spoiled, the fact that she is an only child has meant that she has received a great deal of parental time and affection.

The Youth Club attached to her school has decided to restart discos on Friday evenings after a forced interval of three months. The decision to stop the discos was made by the Youth Club Management Committee after an incident in which a girl was injured in a fight.

All of her friends, in fact most of the girls in her year, are going to go to the first disco on the coming Friday, and obviously, Sylvie is very keen to go.

When she spoke to her parents about it they said that they were unhappy about her going because of the trouble that had occurred at the club previously.

You will now have an opportunity to interview Sylvie's father, Mr Gareth Thomson and Ms Audrey Wood, the Youth Worker who runs the disco and decide whether you think that Sylvie should be allowed to go.

Youth club disco

Mr Gareth Thomson

I am not an over-protective parent. When I was young I used to attend youth clubs and know how important a social life is to young people.

My concern about Sylvie wanting to go to the disco is due to the recent history of trouble at the youth club, particularly on nights when discos have been held. A number of young people are known to have been drunk on those nights, which is not in itself too serious an issue for me, except when their high spirits turn to violence.

The reason the discos were stopped was that on the last occasion, a girl had a bottle smashed on her face causing her to receive stitches.

I do not want to seem like an overbearing parent but I do not want to put my daughter at risk in any way at all.

I believe that the present youth worker, Ms Wood, does not have the experience or support to allow her to run successful and safe discos, and consequently I have told Sylvie that she cannot go.

Youth club disco

Ms Audrey Wood – letter to District Youth Officer

Dear Derek,

    I have decided to re-open the club for discos as from next Friday.

    As you know, I believe that the Management Committee over-reacted when they forced the three month closure on me earlier in the year. The isolated incident that occured, while regrettable, was not really anything to do with this club. The young people concerned had been in a pub disco in town and were a little the worse for drink when they arrived at 9.30 pm. My staff and I realise that we made a mistake in allowing them in and we have learned from that mistake.

    It goes without saying that we are concerned about the safety of young people and it is for this reason we want to restart the disco here at the club. We know that if we do not make this provision, young people will drift into the pubs and clubs in town where they will be inappropriately supervised and where they will be exposed to alcohol and possibly drugs. Much of the violence is also centered on these venues.

    I feel that you will support my decision and I assure you that my staff and I will make every effort to provide the young people with an enjoyable social experience in a safe and supportive environment.

Best wishes,

Audrey Wood

Youth club disco

Written assignments

1 Write Sylvie's diary covering the period of dispute with her parents.

2 Describe and justify the decision that you made about whether or not Sylvie should go to the disco.

3 Imagine the dialogue between Mr Thomson and Ms Wood. Write it either as a play or as a narrative.

4 How much freedom do you believe young people should be given in deciding what they can and cannot do?

Practice Activity 5 Saturday Job

Aim

To introduce simple role play techniques involving shared background information (see page 45) and two role players.

Method

1 The teacher distributes the background sheet and allows time for the pupils to consider questions that they may wish to ask. The question/response pro forma (see page 13) may be used if desired. Pupils may need prompting as to the sort of questions to ask.

2 Either the teacher plus one pupil or two pupils are given the role sheets.

3 The class is divided into two groups and have an opportunity to interview each of the role players in turn.

4 Having interviewed both characters, each group should reach a conclusion and then should share their ideas in a class discussion. In each case, the groups should justify the decision they have made.

Saturday job

Background information

Ian McCoughlin is a fifteen year old boy who attends his local school and wants to be a mechanic when he leaves.

In August at the end of his fourth year, he got a part-time job as an assistant on a green-grocer's stall in the market and he now works every Saturday from 7.00 am until about 5.30 pm. His job involves setting up the stall, selling fruit and vegetables and generally keeping the area around the stall clean and tidy.

He has always found the job hard and he didn't particularly like it, but he is prepared to stick it as he is saving up for a motorbike when he is seventeen.

When he arrived twenty minutes late for work last Saturday his boss, Mr Frank Moss, told him that he wasn't needed any more.

Ian was very upset and told Mr Moss that he thought he was being made a scapegoat.

You now have an opportunity to interview Ian and Mr Moss and decide whether the sacking was fair.

Saturday job

Ian McCoughlin

I have worked really hard when necessary for not very much money. I've had to start work very early and often did not finish until after 6.00 at night. When this happened I was never paid for the extra time. I didn't mind serving the customers but I was always being dragged away to do really heavy or dirty jobs.

I think that Mr Moss treated all of the part-time staff very badly and loved to show people up in front of the customers. He has been particularly hard on some of us lately and I think that it's because trade has fallen off quite a lot recently.

He used my being late as an excuse for sacking me. He did it in front of all of the other staff. This really upset me and I called him a few names. I know I shouldn't have done that but I felt really angry.

Even though I don't want to work for him any more I feel that being sacked will go against me if I apply for another job.

Saturday job

Mr Frank Moss

You have always employed young lads on your stall and you have never had the problems with others as you have had with Ian. He was OK at first but particularly since he started back at school his mind has not been on the job.

You don't pay a fortune but no less than any other stalls on the market. You don't expect anyone to work every minute of the day but you do think it reasonable that people turn up on time, and Ian was often late. This was not your main complaint, though. You often had to tell Ian to stop gossiping with his friends who came by and on a number of occasions, you had to go find him after sending him on simple errands.

You warned him at least four times and when he was late last Saturday, it was the last straw. The language he came out with was appalling and only confirmed your view that he should be sacked. There are always plenty of people who are keen to earn a few pounds on Saturdays.

Saturday job

Written assignments

1 Ian McCoughlin applies for another job and is forced to name Mr Moss as a referee. Write the reference that Mr Moss will send. (Note: references are written in very special language.)

2 Describe a typical day for Ian at the market stall.

3 *All young people should experience the world of work while still at school.* To what extent do you agree with this.

4 Ian decides that he was wrong to have reacted in the way that he did. Write his letter of apology to Mr Moss asking for re-employment.

Practise Activity 6 School Residential

Aim

To introduce simple role play techniques involving shared background information (see page 50) and four role players.

Method

1 The teacher distributes the background sheet and allows time for the pupils to consider questions that they may wish to ask. The question/response pro forma (see page 12) may be used if desired. Pupils may need prompting as to the sort of questions to ask.
2 Either the teacher plus three pupils or four pupils are given the role sheets.
3 The class is divided into four groups and have an opportunity to interview each of the role players in turn.
4 Having interviewed both characters, each group should reach a conclusion and then should share their ideas in a class discussion. In each case, the groups should justify the decision they have made.

School residential

Background information

Karen Kelly is due to leave St Bede's High School next Easter and has asked to go on the School Leavers' residential course in February. This course happens each year and is intended to give school leavers an experience of working other than in a classroom. One of the important requirements is the ability to share living accommodation for three days.

Sandra Willetts is another pupil who is due to go on the course and she has approached the teacher in charge, Mr Paul Ormerod, to tell him that a number of the pupils are unhappy about Karen being allowed to go. They fear that she will be disruptive during the sessions and generally cause trouble.

Sandra is supported by Mr Eric Hardy, the Head of Fifth Year at the School. He has had a lot of dealings with Karen Kelly and finds her difficult.

Karen is very keen to go and sees it as her last opportunity to get something from school.

You will now have a chance to speak to all of the characters involved and to decide whether or not Karen should be allowed to join the course.

The people you will meet are:

> Karen Kelly
> Sandra Willetts
> Mr Paul Ormerod – teacher in charge
> Mr Eric Hardy – Head of Fifth Year

School residential

Karen Kelly

You don't think that school has given you very much. Because you find examination work difficult, some people think that you do not like school. You always seem to be the one blamed when things go wrong and although your behaviour isn't perfect, you are always singled out.

You know people who went on the course last year and they really enjoyed it. Mr Ormerod made a point of inviting you to apply for the course and you are looking forward to it.

When you heard about what Sandra Willetts said you didn't hide your anger when you next saw her. You believe that she has no right to get you thrown off the course. You are not surprised about Mr Hardy's attitude, he has never shown any concern for you and has always picked on you.

School residential

Sandra Willetts

You have been looking forward to this course for ages but when you heard that Karen Kelly was going you and your friends were put off. You think that this course is for people who have worked hard and have contributed to the school in the past, not for people who fool about and cause trouble. She never takes work seriously in class so how on earth would she take any interest in this?

Added to that, the idea of having to spend three whole days with her, instead of just a few lessons, would ruin it for you.

You are not the only one to think like this and you know that if she is allowed to go, a number of you will drop out.

School residential

Mr Paul Ormerod

Sandra Willetts and her friends have shown themselves to be very selfish over this matter of Karen coming on the residential course. While you understand their concerns about Karen's past behaviour, they forget the course is designed for everybody irrespective of how well they have done in school.

In the past, pupils have had differences that the residential course has helped solve. You know that Karen has been a handful in the classroom but you feel that she will respond well to the residential environment and gain a great deal from it.

Your hope is that Sandra will calm down and accept that Karen is going. If she feels that she cannot come because Karen will be there, then it is her loss.

School residential

Mr Eric Hardy

You have had a number of dealings with the Kelly girl and her elder brothers and sisters over the years. They are a bad lot and give nothing to the school.

You have heard that she wants to go on the residential course and that a number of the nicer pupils have objected. You are not surprised. You would not like to have to spend three days in her company.

This course should be seen as a reward for effort and cooperation not a right. You know that Mr Ormerod does not agree with this point of view but this does not surprise you as you do not see eye to eye about a number of matters, particularly relating to discipline.

You feel that he should listen to the opinions expressed by Sandra and her friends and if it comes to a choice, take them rather than Karen Kelly.

School residential

Written assignments

1 Describe the confrontation between Karen Kelly and Sandra Willetts.

2 Write the conversation between Sandra and Mr Ormerod concerning Karen going on the course.

3 Karen's mother is annoyed that Karen may be prevented from going on the course. Write the letter that she would send to the school.

4 What do you think are the advantages of residential education?

5 *School is not only for those who do well in examinations.* In your experience, how successful are schools in achieving this?

Practice Activity 7 Leaving School

Aim

To introduce simple role play techniques involving shared background information and four role players.

Method

1 The teacher distributes the background sheet and allows time for the pupils to consider questions that they may wish to ask. The question/response pro forma may be used if desired. Pupils may need prompting as to the sort of questions to ask.
2 Four pupils are given the role sheets.
3 The class is divided into four groups and have an opportunity to interview each of the role players in turn.
4 Having interviewed both characters, each group should reach a conclusion and then should share their ideas in a class discussion. In each case, the groups should justify the decision they have made.

Leaving school

Background information

Angela is waiting for the results of her GCSE examinations in English Language, English Literature, Mathematics, History, Geography, French, Biology and Art. Her teachers expect her to do very well in all of her subjects.

She lives with her parents and her twenty year old sister, Phillipa and her younger brother. Her father works at the Town Hall and her mother works part-time at the local Citizen's Advice Bureau.

Her form-tutor, Mr Glen Wilde, is very keen that she stays on at school and does 'A' levels and goes on to University.

She is, however, uncertain what to do with her future. She knows that with the qualifications that she is likely to get, she would have little difficulty in getting work when she leaves school. On the other hand, she enjoys some aspects of school work and finds learning quite easy.

You have the opportunity to speak to the people most involved in her decision. These will be:

> Miss Phillipa Clayton – her sister
> Mr Alan Clayton – her father
> Mrs Sarah Clayton – her mother
> Mr Glenn Wilde – her form tutor

When you have interviewed each of them in turn, you will have to make a recommendation as to what Angela should do.

Leaving school

Phillipa Clayton

You left school at 16 with five 'O' levels and you are glad that you did. You enjoy your job with Nat West and you have already had a promotion giving you enough money to run a car. You have a good social life and you have no regrets about leaving school when you did.

Your mother is really ambitious and pushed you very hard to stay at school as she is now doing with Angela. You've talked to Angela and you are convinced that if it was left up to her, she would leave school also.

Schools always want people to stay on but there are other ways of spending your time and doing well for yourself.

Leaving school

Mr Alan Clayton

You have been pleased at the success that your daughters have had at school but you do not believe that there would be any real advantages to Angela staying on to do 'A' level. After all, how much better would the job be that she took at 18?

You left school at 15 and you have done very well for yourself and your family. Your son is likely to continue the record of success and he hopes to get a commission in the forces. You can understand him wanting to stay on because he needs the qualifications, but Angela doesn't.

You know that your wife is keen for Angela to stay at school but you don't see the point. She may well be married by the time she is twenty-one and what good would her qualifications be then?

Leaving school

Mrs Sarah Clayton

Your husband's attitude infuriates you. As far as he is concerned, qualifications are important for men but useless for women.

Phillipa had to work very hard for her five 'O' levels but Angela finds academic work enjoyable and easier. Although Phillipa had the chance to go on, you feel that you didn't give her enough encouragement at the time and although she seems to be doing all right, you can't help but feel that she missed an opportunity by not doing the 'A' level course.

Angela has a good brain but at the moment she does not realise how far she could go, nor how important it is for women in particular to get qualifications in order to succeed in a man's world.

You would be very unhappy if she left school to work in an office where her abilities would be wasted.

Leaving school

Mr Glenn Wilde

Angela is one of the brightest girls that you have ever taught and you have high hopes for her. You have told her many times that she would be making a serious mistake by not doing 'A' levels, a mistake that she would regret for the rest of her life.

Her sister, although moderately bright, never showed Angela's potential but you were nevertheless disappointed with her decision to leave school.

You are aware of the views of Mr Clayton and you deplore them. You feel sure that if he had a son, he would give him maximum encouragement to stay on at school and then go on to University.

You are determined that Angela should be allowed that opportunity.

Leaving school

Written assignments

1 *The only way to success is through qualifications.* To what extent is this true?

2 Angela chooses to leave school and names Mr Wilde as a referee. Write the reference that he would send.

3 Describe and justify the advice given by your group to Angela.

4 Angela decides to stay on at school. Describe the conversation with her family when she announces the decision.

6 ROLE-PLAYS

Jonathan Banks

Teacher's notes

Jonathan Banks presents a scenario which most pupils find very easy to identify with – most schools have a few boys very much like Jonathan.

The roles also present few difficulties, with the possible exception of the Probation Officer, Janis Carpenter and for this reason her evidence can either be presented by an experienced role-player (possibly the teacher), or in its written form, see the memo on page 74. The boy who plays Harry Banks will have to infer from the transcript of the conversation the attitude that he has towards the circumstances of the case and the desirable outcome. It may need to be emphasised that the Probation Officer has strong reservations about the suitability of Harry Banks, he is not an ideal foster father!

All of the options listed in the Background Information sheet have supporters who clearly justify the reasons for their decisions.

In practice, one feature of the role-play has not had too much attention focussed on it, the possible racist motive for the attack on the shop. Although pupils in the trial school received some preliminary sessions on race related issues, little attention was drawn to that aspect of the evidence presented in the Background Information sheet and the newspaper report. Teachers wishing to do so must feel satisfied that this particular role-play is a suitable vehicle for exploring possible racist motives for attacks of this kind. This is not to say that schools should ignore the issue and the authors fully endorse the view expressed in the Swann report:

> If in the face of such forms of racism, or in the face of ignorance and inaccurate statements about ethnic minorities, the school seeks simply to remain neutral and uninvolved, we would see this as not only a failure in terms of its educational responsibilities but also as in effect condoning and thereby encouraging the persistence of such occurrences. (Swann p. 35)

It may be that teachers would wish to use the attack in *Jonathan Banks* as a starting point to allow pupils to explore at a later date their attitudes to such events.

Jonathan Banks

Background information

Jonathan Banks is a fourteen year old boy who is in the fourth year at his local comprehensive school. He lives with his mother and father and three younger brothers, one of whom attends the same school. His father works as a machine operator in a paper mill and his mother cleans at the nearby primary school.

His primary school records show that he was an average all-round pupil who mixed well and his first five terms at Crompton Park High School were trouble free. After Easter of the second year, however, he was a changed boy. He became abusive to members of staff, started truanting and perhaps worst of all, began associating with a group of older boys who were known to be responsible for causing disturbances which had brought them into contact with the local police.

In September of his third year he appeared before the local magistrates accused of criminal damage and theft for which he was fined £250 and placed on probation for twelve months.

During the Christmas holidays he and two other members of his group were arrested for setting fire to a local shop. Although no-one was injured, the shop was gutted and the owners believe that there was a racist motive for the attack.

Jonathan is now appearing before the magistrates for sentencing and you have to advise them on a suitable course of action.

Your alternatives include:

> A custodial sentence;
> Being placed in the care of the local authority;
> A further fine and/or period of probation;
> A Community Service Order;
> A Residential School for young offenders.

You will be able to get evidence from the following people:

> Mr and Mrs Banks – Parents
> Mr Michael Gillies – Youth Worker
> Mrs Valerie Masters – Headteacher
> Mr Harry Banks – Uncle
> Ms Janis Carpenter – Probation Officer

before you make your recommendation.

© Mike Davis and Tim Long 1989. Basil Blackwell Ltd.

Jonathan Banks

Further notes

Custodial sentence

For someone of Jonathan's age, a custodial sentence would be a period of Youth Custody, often called *a short, sharp shock*. The period of detention can range from 3 months to 2 years. Youth custody is organised on military lines and involves work, strenuous physical exercise and education. Young people who are sentenced to youth custody are highly likely to reoffend. The National Association for the Care of Resettlement of Offenders (NACRO) report that between 70 and 80% of young people given custodial sentences will reoffend within two years of release.

Care

This means that the responsibility for the upbringing of a young person is transferred from the parents to the Local Authority. A child in this situation would first spend a period of time in an Assessment Centre before being allocated. In practice a child in care can:

> remain at home with parents but subject to a Social Worker;
> be put up for fostering;
> be placed in a children's home.

In each case, a social worker takes over responsibility until the young person reaches the age of 18 years.

Probation

A person placed on probation has to report frequently to a Probation Officer. Conditions may be placed on movement and contacts with certain people. There can also be a requirement to attend group sessions with Probation Officers and other offenders.

Community Service Order

A Community Order forces an offender to work in activities of benefit to the community under the supervision of the Probation Service. These are often physical activities like clearing public spaces, gardening, decorating etc and can last up to 240 hours,

Jonathan Banks

Further notes, *continued*

usually a few hours per week out of school or working time. Failure to attend or to do the work satisfactorily can mean being returned to court for an alternative sentence.

Residential school for young offenders

Some Local Authorities provide residential education for young people if their offences have an effect on their ability to perform well at school. The young people receive normal schooling and plenty of opportunities to learn other skills outside of normal school hours. They also have to take domestic responsibilities like cleaning, washing up etc. They earn privileges by good behaviour.

Jonathan Banks

Mr and Mrs Banks

You have worked hard to give your children all of the opportunities that you never had. When Jonathan was younger, he never caused any problems and he never resented having to take responsibility for his younger brothers when mother started work.

Recently, however, many arguments have arisen at home, he insists on staying out late, he uses appalling language, and you suspect that he has been stealing money from the house, all of which you find shocking. Also you now find it impossible to communicate with him and you do not understand how he has got into so much trouble. It may have something to do with the boys he spends his time with, but you worry that it is something in him.

Your concern now is that his behaviour might have an effect on the younger members of the family, who all seem to be good boys. You feel that you can no longer put up with his behaviour and if he is to continue like this, it will have to be somewhere other than your own home.

Jonathan Banks

Youth worker – Mr Michael Gillies

You've known Jonathan Banks for about three years, from when he started coming to the junior club, and when he brought his younger brothers to the playschemes during school holidays. He has not been in the club much since Easter, except for a few Friday night discos when he turned up with some older lads who you've known for five or six years and who are, quite frankly, trouble.

You think that Jonathan's recent misbehaviour is a direct result of associating with these young people, and if he could be weaned away from them, he'd be OK. You think that it's just a phase he's going through. You've seen this sort of thing happen before and it's essential that people don't get carried away in their judgements about him.

He had too much responsibility given to him when he was too young, and his parents have put a lot of pressure on him to behave in an acceptable way. You consider his recent behaviour a reaction against this.

Jonathan Banks

Headmistress – Mrs Valeria Masters

You see Banks as one of those aggressive boys who seems intent on disruption. He is much larger than other third years and he has been involved in a number of incidents of bullying and extortion of money from younger and smaller children.

You believe that the teaching staff at Crompton Park High School are sympathetic to the needs of all pupils, regardless of ability, but Banks does not even meet you half way. You have found him to be rude to staff and pupils, uncooperative and disruptive.

You do not consider him to be fit for normal schooling and believe that he is in need of a stricter environment.

Jonathan Banks

Compton Park High School

Memorandum

To: District Education Officer
From: Headmistress, Crampton Park High School

re: Jonathan Banks

1. I am writing to inform you that Jonathan Banks is currently being considered for suspension following a series of incidents viz bullying, extortion of money from younger children, and more recently, his arrest for allegedly being involved in an attack on a local shop.

2. I would add that Banks has tried the patience of staff at this school who have made every effort to treat him sympathetically. I personally have found him to be aggressive on the few occasions that I have had to deal with him.

3. As you know, I have to cater for the interests of all the pupils and the continued presence of Banks is not in their best interests either socially or educationally. He should be found an alternative place as soon as possible.

V. Masters

V. Masters
Headmistress

Jonathan Banks

Mr Harry Banks – Uncle

You have always had a special affection for your first nephew, particularly as you have never married yourself. You know that he has been in trouble, but what normal lad hasn't? Your brother and sister-in-law expect him to behave in a responsible way, looking after the younger boys, but will not recognise that he is no longer a kid himself.

There have been arguments with your brother when you have taken Jonathan for a few drinks even though you and he used to go with your father at Jonathan's age. You sense that your brother resents your friendship with Jonathan because you seem to be able to talk to him when he can't.

You feel that he would much rather stay with you than go back to his parents. You believe that, given the chance, you could make a man of him and keep him out of trouble. You would be willing to take responsibility for him if this could be arranged.

Jonathan Banks

Transcript of conversation between Harry Banks and Fergus Slater

(Harry and Fergus are in their local pub talking about Jonathan.)

Harry: Well it's happened again. Jon's up to his neck in it.
Fergus: What is it this time?
Harry: He set fire to a shop, so they say. He said that he and his mates were just messing about and now he's got to go to court again.
Fergus: That's a shame . . .
Harry: You know what really gets on my nerves don't you, is the way his parents treat him. I've told you before, they're always expecting him to do too much. It's no way to bring up a lad expecting him to wash up and cook meals and that. And anyway, for heaven's sake, what's his dad up to? We never had to do that when we were young and it's a load of rubbish when he says that Jon is badly behaved. I mean, he was a bit of a lad himself, but he never mentions that, does he now.
Fergus: What do you mean?
Harry: We used to go drinking when we were Jon's age and do you remember that time I brought him in here? Well when they found out, they went up the wall. Especially his mother. I think it's her. She treats him like a little girl. I mean it's her job to look after the house not Jon's. You know what they're thinking about doing?
Fergus: What?
Harry: Getting rid of him, aren't they. Sending him away. Fine parents they've turned out to be. Now I know I've no kids, but I can tell you this, I'd give him a better home than they have. And you know something, I think he would like the idea of staying with me. At least I'd bring him up to be a man.
Fergus: Have you suggested it?
Harry: Yeh. And I've spoken to his probation officer but I haven't heard from her yet. His parents are not that keen though.

Jonathan Banks

Probation officer – Ms Janis Carpenter

While recognising that Jonathan seems to be a troublesome boy, your contacts with him during your supervision of his probation lead you to believe that the responsibility for this latest incident is not as clear cut as first appearances might suggest. You see him very much as a victim of a series of inaccurate judgements:

a) his parents have expected far too much from him, he looks mature, but is not, and the responsibilities they have given him over the last three years have put him under unfair pressure;

b) his school have all too readily labelled him as troublesome. They have been insensitive to his needs, both social and educational, and all too concerned about the image of the school;

c) his role in the previous offence, has been over-emphasised. His co-defendants, all aged 17, exploited his immaturity and his eagerness to please, a fact that was given little credence by the bench.

You are concerned about Jonathan's relationship with his uncle, Harry Banks. Although you appreciate his interest and affection for Jonathan, you recognise that their relationship is causing anger and resentment in his immediate family, thus frustrating attempts to improve relationships in the parental home.

Jonathan Banks

MEMO

re: Jonathan Banks

While recognising that Jonathan seems to be a
troublesome boy, my contacts with him
during the earlier supervision of his
probation lead me to believe that the
responsibility for this latest incident is not
as clear cut as first appearances might suggest.
I see him very much as a victim of a series of
inaccurate judgements:

a) his parents have expected far too much from
him - he looks mature, but he is not, and the
responsibilities they have given him over the
last three years have put him under unfair
pressure;

b) his school have all too readily labelled
him as troublesome. They have been insensitive
to his needs, both social and educational, and
all too concerned about the image of the school;

c) his role in the previous offence, has been
over-emphasised. His co-defendants in this most
recent case, all aged 17, exploited his
immaturity and his eagerness to please - a
fact that I would like to stress in my report.

I am concerned about Jonathan's relationship
with his uncle, Harry Banks. Although I
appreciate his interest and affection for
Jonathan, I believe that their relationship
is causing anger and resentment in his
immediate family. He has offered a home for
Jonathan and before I complete my final report
for the court this option needs to be discussed

J. Carpenter

I'le see you about this Friday A.M.
John Mason.

Jonathan Banks

Report from local newspaper

LOCAL SHOP GUTTED

Five Youths arrested

Local shopkeepers Mr and Mrs Hussain narrowly escaped serious injury when a group of hooligans set fire to their shop late last night causing considerable damage to the property. An eye-witness said a large group of teenage boys were causing trouble all night. 'My husband went out three times to try and clear them away but all he got was abuse. We eventually phoned the police but this was after we saw the shop burning.' The Fire Brigade managed to limit the damage to the shop and no other properties were damaged. 'This is the fifth incident of this type in the last six weeks,' said Divisional Fire Officer John Grant. 'It seems that a group of older boys are encouraging younger ones to engage in serious criminal damage. It is only luck that nobody has been killed.'

Mrs Hussain told our reporter that there was a racist motive for this attack. 'This group of youths have caused a lot of trouble for us recently. They have shouted abuse and have sprayed obscenities on the outside of the shop. I hope that the courts deal severely with them.'

The youths arrested were released on bail to appear in court early next week.

Jonathan Banks

Written assignments

1 Imagine that you are Ms Janis Carpenter. Write your report assessing what you think to be the most suitable course of action for the magistrates to take.

2 Describe the problems that Jonathan Banks experiences. Attempt to account for the different ways that different people regard him.

3 Write an account of One Day in the Life of Jonathan Banks.

4 Write a newspaper account of the fire-bombing of Mr and Mrs Hussain's shop. Remember to include comments made by local residents and any possible witnesses as well as the Police.

5 What difficulties do young people experience during adolescence? Write a magazine article of about 600 words.

6 Write a play about Jonathan's trial in the Juvenile Court. In addition to the characters you have already met, you may need to include other witnesses.

Dave Marshall

Teacher's notes

Dave Marshall needs to be placed firmly in context of medical definitions of 'brain death'. The following notes were compiled after careful reading and consultation with the Director of an Intensive Care Unit in a large London Hospital:

> A patient is currently defined as dead when brain stem death has occurred. The brain stem, which comprises the midbrain, pons and medulla oblongata, controls the body's vital functions such as breathing. Once this has been destroyed it is impossible for the patient to regain consciousness although s/he may be supported by an artificial ventilator. This, however, can only be a temporary measure, as a cardiovascular or 'heart' failure will inevitably be the ultimate outcome of such medical treatment. Consequently, such a course of action is considered pointless and the removal of the patient from the ventilator presents no ethical dilemma to the medical team.
>
> The ethical dilemma does, however, become more complex in the case of irreversible cerebral damage. If the brain stem stays intact but the cerebral cortex stops functioning a patient may breath spontaneously and survive for a long period of time but in a vegetative state. Such a dilemma is intensified when the patient is more than vegetative but badly disabled. Clearly, such situations pose far greater ethical difficulties.
>
> It should be borne in mind that the diagnosis of brain steam death can only be reached after an extensive and rigorously controlled series of medical tests.

The experience of role-playing *Dave Marshall* is a solemn one. The young people identify very closely with the dilemma faced by the members of the family, particularly if there has been a similar case or cases in the neighbourhood of the school. For that reason, it would be well advised to ensure that nobody in the class has suffered the loss of a member of the family in similar or other circumstances.

Dr Shahida Maqsood and Fr Hugo Sullivan can both present problems for unskilled role-players and consequently their evidence may be better presented in its written form. In our experience, the problem seems to stem not from an inability to grasp the issues but from an unfamiliarity with the appropriate register. On one occasion a very skilled 16 year old suffered the role of Fr Sullivan and commented afterwards that he couldn't get the religious tone quite right. This was clearly due to his limited experience of priests and

Dave Marshall

Teacher's notes

clerics who in our researches seemed to us to speak in the same way as other professionals rather than some TV generated stereotype. Perhaps pupils who are in regular contact with churchmen would not experience the same degree of difficulty. His problem, however, could have been anticipated and his concerns allayed by asking him simply to play it as a concerned professional, something that, in our experience, young people are quite capable of doing.

Dave Marshall

Background information

WIFE'S ANGUISH OVER LIFE-SUPPORT

Local wife, Leanne Marshall today faces the worst decision of her life – should she tell the doctors to switch off the machine that is keeping her husband alive.

Mr Dave Marshall, age twenty-nine, has been on the life-support machine at St Anne's Hospital after being involved in a head-on collision with a lorry on the A6 on Tuesday of last week. Mrs Marshall, who has two children aged five and seven, must now decide whether to agree to the medical advice given her that, as her husband is brain dead, the best course of action is to turn off the life-support machine.

She is at present being comforted by relatives and is being guided by the parish priest.

Using the information given above, you now have the opportunity to discover the views of these following people:

> Mrs Leanne Marshall – Dave's wife
> Dr Shahida Maqsood – Consultant Neurologist
> Mr and Mrs Marshall – Dave's parents
> Fr Hugo Sullivan SJ – Family Priest
> Mr Peter Marshall – Dave's brother

after which you will be asked to make a recommendation about the course of action that Leanne Marshall should take.

Dave Marshall

Mrs Leanne Marshall – Dave's wife

It was seven o'clock in the evening when you heard that Dave had been involved in the crash and that was the beginning of the worst few days of your life. When you went to the hospital you were told that Dave was undergoing surgery to remove a blood clot from his brain and that the doctors had expressed some optimism about his chances of recovery.

After these initial hopeful signs, however, Dave's condition deteriorated and he went into a coma. You found the whole situation unbearable and struggled to grasp the full horror, the prospect of bringing up your children without a father, the loss of a livelihood and worst of all, the loss of your husband.

It was in this state of utter dismay that the doctors told you that Dave had suffered brain death, that he was only alive because of the life support system. You were told that in their opinion, there was no hope of Dave coming out of the coma and even in the unlikely event of his doing so, he would be a 'vegetable' for the rest of his life.

The doctors have asked for your approval to switch off the machine but now you are in such an emotional turmoil and so devastated by what has happened that you feel unable to make that decision. You understand what they are saying but cannot bring yourself to be actually responsible for terminating his life. You feel unable to make a rational judgement about the situation because of the love you feel for Dave. You know deep down that it is the right thing to switch off the machine, but it is such a final step, and one that would be with you for the rest of your life, that you are unable to take it.

Dave Marshall

Letter from Dr Shahida Maqsood to Mr and Mrs Marshall

St Anne's Hospital

Dear Mr and Mrs Marshall

Thank you for your letter received today. As
I said to you last week, these situations are
always difficult and while the medical position
is always clear, the human dilemma is always
traumatic. Your son's injuries were extensive;
he had lost a great deal of blood and there
were serious fractures of the skull causing
depressions in the brain. It is my firm
medical belief that the extent of his injuries
have killed him, for although he is still
clinically alive, his brain is dead.

Though the advances made in medical science
would allow us to keep him alive when we
consider the quality of life that we would be
maintaining, it is clear that we would be
doing little more than keeping the organs of
his body functioning. Life after brain death
is not life as it is intended. A body merely
functioning without any sense or sensation,
cannot be the desired end-product of medical
intervention.

We wish to make it clear that were we to keep
the life support machine in operation, your son
would never regain consciousness, and would be
forever dependent on the machine sustaining
him. He would be unable to leave the hospital
and the likely prognosis is a slow but sure
deterioration of his major organs leading to
inevitable death at an indeterminate time in
the future.

I understand the awful decision that faces
your family and you have my every sympathy. In
issues of life and death there are never any
easy solutions. Personally, I hate having to
suggest such a course of action but profession-
ally I know that it is my duty to advise you to
agree to shut down the system. Of course, the
decision lies with your daughter-in-law and I
hope you will be able to support her in making
the correct choice.

If you would like to discuss further, please
do not hesitate to contact me.

Yours sincerely,

S. Maqsood.

Dave Marshall

Mr and Mrs Marshall – Dave's parents

You refuse to accept the conclusion that David is dead. You see the heartbeat monitored on the life support machine and can see him breathing. You know that some people don't place a high value on human life but as Christians you cannot condone any action that would lead to a person's death. To suggest that the machine should be switched off is monstrous and you cannot understand Leanne's confusion and uncertainty. If she loves him as much as she says, then the last thing in the world she would want would be to allow the doctors to bring about his death by turning off the machine. You believe that this is only a little short of murder.

To you, in the eyes of God, life is sacred and it is your Christian duty to maintain the sanctity of life. By turning off the life support machine you would break one of the most fundamental aspects of your faith.

You recognise that this is a terrible time for Leanne as it is for all of you. You are upset, however, that Leanne has seemed unable to control her emotions and recognise what has to be done. She doesn't seem to understand that even if she has to look after David for the rest of her life, that is her wifely duty.

The doctor has given a medical verdict and has advised accordingly, but while you see life in David, you cannot under any circumstances accept this. David must be helped to live and not to die.

Dave Marshall

Father Hugo Sullivan SJ – extract from a sermon

Before I close, I want to say a little about the plight of David Marshall and his family, who I am sure you have all heard or read about.

Contrary to popular opinion, we in the Church are realistic about these situations for both practical and theological reasons.

From a practical point of view, we recognise that medical science can only do so much, and if a doctor says that there is no real chance of recovery, that must be accepted.

From a theological point of view, the issue is one of an acceptance of the afterlife and an acknowledgement that heaven is a better place than earth.

We all understand and sympathise with David's family and our role is to help them, through prayer, to reach the decision with which they can live and also to recognise that death on earth is the beginning of a better life in heaven.

Dave Marshall

Mr Peter Marshall – Dave's brother

You have always been close to Dave and get on very well with Leanne. His accident was a devastating blow and you feel that you are only beginning to come to terms with it. You believe that you are the only one in the family who has got a clear view of the dilemma and to you there is only one answer – to switch off the machine.

You know that there is no chance of Dave ever recovering and your concern now is to ease the situation for Leanne and the children, something that Dave would have wanted anyway. You feel that Leanne is being made to feel unduly guilty by your parents whose religious beliefs you have never sympathised with. You are not without your own beliefs and it is these that lead you to think that it is the easing of the suffering that is most important. To accuse her of a lack of love for him is a travesty of the truth. She has been put through enough already without having this additional burden forced upon her.

Dave Marshall

Written assignments

1 Write the conversation between Leanne and Dave's parents when the full extent of Dave's injuries becomes apparent. You can, if you wish, write it as a play and include any of the other characters.

2 Describe the consequences of your decision on Leanne's daily life two years into the future.

3 *It is the responsibility of medicine to support life whenever it is possible.* Explore this statement with close reference to the case of Dave Marshall and other similar cases you may have read or heard about.

4 What steps do you consider could and should be taken to reduce death and injury on the road? Write a newspaper feature article of between 600 and 1000 words.

5 Imagine you are the driver of the lorry that crashed into Dave Marshall's car. Write a letter to Leanne explaining how you feel.

Parkside Road High School

Teacher's notes

At this time of falling rolls and financial stringency, Parkside Road High School is probably typical of at least one school in every LEA in the country and as such, it is likely that there will be contemporary newspaper reports available to provide a context for this role-play. An interesting feature about school closure was identified by an anonymous Chief Education Officer who is reported to have commented:

> Unpopular schools are usually unpopular for good reasons and are thus ideal targets for closure when falling rolls hit an area. The curiosity is that as soon as a school is identified as unpopular, and therefore a contender for closure, it ceases to be unpopular and supporters emerge from all sections of the community. It is for this reason that school closure presents so many difficulties for LEAs.

LEA difficulties notwithstanding it is evident that most schools generate considerable loyalty among pupils past and present, parents, staff (teaching and non-teaching) and shops and houses in their localities. Arising from this loyalty emerges a wide variety of local action committees which could form the basis of a more extended simulation if the circumstances arose. While Parkside Road is a fictitious institution and all of the characters are inventions, the use of this role-play was considerably enhanced by the intended closure of the school where the materials were trialled.

Parkside Road High School

Background information

Parkside Road High School was built in 1966 to serve a large council estate at the southern end of a borough in the Midlands. Originally, it was planned to have a pupil population of about 600. Because of an increase in local population in the 1970s, the school expanded to nearly 1200 pupils and additional classroom accommodation was built.

From its earliest days the school never enjoyed a good reputation, either for success in academic terms or for the behaviour of its pupils.

Among the effects of the 1980 and 1988 Education Acts was the right of parents to have much more choice about where their children were educated. This, combined with a national trend of falling rolls, meant certain schools being considered for closure. Parkside Road is one of these.

You will come across the views of the following people before you make a decision as to whether to begin the formal process of closure required under the 1980 Education Act No. 2:

> Mrs Dawn Richardson – Headteacher
> Councillor Peter Franklin – Vice-Chairman of
>   Education Committee
> Mr Stephen Compton – Chief Education Officer
> Mr Gerry Kubacki – Teacher
> Ms Stephanie Williams – Community Worker
> Mr and Mrs Anderson – ex-pupils

Parkside Road High School

Transcript of a speech by Headteacher Mrs D. Richardson to the Parents Action Committee

As you know, I have been Headteacher of Parkside Road High School for a little over four years and have been impressed by the quality of the work of staff and pupils. I have struggled to change the public image of the school and impress upon people that despite its problems it is a caring institution that has been in the forefront of a number of extremely exciting educational initiatives.

I would like to remind you about the issues that the school faces:

1 The state of disrepair. The design and construction of the school is inappropriate to its location and consequently it requires extensive work to bring it to an acceptable state. The local authority have failed to carry out routine maintenance over the years and parts of the school are in a severe state of delapidation. This has put off prospective parents.

2 The needs of the pupils. Many pupils come to Parkside Road with a variety of learning problems which the school feels that it successfully overcomes.

3 Its poor reputation which reflects the public preoccupation with defining a school, only in terms of examination success, ignoring the fact that there are other means of assessing the achievements of a school.

I believe that the decision to consider the closure of Parkside Road High School is based on false comparisons with other High Schools in the area and that the Authority is all too willing to equate success simply with examination results. It is my firm belief that all of our pupils should be given the opportunity to succeed in their own terms, irrespective of their academic ability. This is what Parkside Road High School has done and it should be on these terms that it is judged.

I hope you give full support to the activities of the **Parents' Against Closure Committee** for without all your help, your school will be lost.

© Mike Davis and Tim Long 1989. Basil Blackwell Ltd.

Parkside Road High School

Councillor Peter Franklin – Vice-Chairman Education Committee

Parkside Road High School is certainly not a school that you would want your child to go to. You have visited the school on a number of occasions and are appalled at the lack of discipline and the state of the buildings, which have obviously been the target for vandalism and graffiti. It is patently obvious that the school is not succeeding which a glance at the examination results makes all to clear.

The fact that parents in this area are voting with their feet and sending their children to other schools makes clear what they think of it.

You have talked to the Headmistress and some of her staff on a number of occasions and you have been struck by their all too ready acceptance of low standards justified on the basis of allowing children to fulfil their own potential. These trendy solutions do not give children what they need and it is clear to you that they do not work anyway. Those other schools that use the more traditional methods, considered authoritarian by the likes of Mrs Richardson have proved their worth time and time again as their examination results show.

You believe that the closure of the school will serve a number of functions:

1 put the children from this area in schools that have a tradition of success rather than failure;
2 save the Authority a considerable amount of money which can be spent on schools that are succeeding; and
3 reduce the number of surplus school places in the area.

Parkside Road High School

Report to the Education Committee from Chief Education Officer

As the Committee knows the main problem facing Local Education Authorities at this time of falling rolls and government financial constraints is to maximise the efficiency of the service. This can only be done by closing schools that are unpopular and expensive to maintain.

I am obliged to give you proper advice as responsible, elected members of the Council. I have therefore compiled a list of schools that could be closed and the criteria I used were:

1. schools that do not have the confidence of local parents, who choose to send their children to schools outside their immediate area:

2. schools that fail to give pupils the opportunity for success at examination level and subsequent transfer into further and higher education; and

3. schools whose buildings are expensive to maintain, for whatever reason.

I regret to say that Parkside Road High School meets all of these criteria all too easily and I therefore have little hesitation in recommending its closure.

Stephen Compton
Stephen Compton
Chief Education Officer

© Mike Davis and Tim Long 1989. Basil Blackwell Ltd.

Parkside Road High School

Mr Gerry Kubacki – Teacher

You have taught at Parkside Road High School for five years after a number of years' experience in so-called successful institutions. In your opinion these schools gain success for a few at the expense of a good education for the many. It is not enough to judge a school by how many of its pupils get good GCSE passes. After all, the GCSE is only intended for the top 60% of the ability range and less than a third of them are likely to get what are the equivalent of 'O' level passes.

You know that the vast majority of pupils cannot be expected to succeed in these terms and a school is obliged to provide educational opportunities for all pupils of whatever ability. Your fear is that through the closure of Parkside Road High School many pupils will not be given the educational environment that will allow them to develop their true potential.

Parkside Road High School has developed a curriculum that is specifically designed to meet the needs of the children who come to it. Children need room and opportunity to develop from where they are, not from where school expects them to be and they also need to be given recognition for what they can do, which might not be judged by examinations. There is more to ability than being successful in examinations. It is your belief that for a lot of the children you deal with, examinations are not appropriate. Rather than simply condemn them to a watered down version of academic work, you actively seek opportunities to develop whatever abilities they possess and give access to opportunities to acquire others. The politicians and the public need to recognise that examination success does not define educational success.

Parkside Road High School

Ms Stephanie Williams – Community Worker

Your view of schools is that they should, as far as possible, serve the community. You have had a long-running involvement with Parkside Road High School and consider that it has the potential to play a significant role in the future of the area. You have seen the benefit of the daytime Adult Student Programme with creche and have fully supported the way the school has opened up its facilities for the community in the evening.

It strikes you as ironic that while a wide range of Local Government services are increasing their commitment to the area, the largest single resource, the school, is being considered for closure. This inconsistency is highlighted by the fact that the County Council is making new Library and Day Nursery provision with one hand, and taking away the High School with the other.

Your contacts with local people convince you that a new future exists for Parkside Road High School and contrary to public opinion, members of the community already value the school highly and see this proposed closure as another indication of the general insensitivity to the needs of the area. Among other things, the closure of the school will mean that pupils will have to travel at least two miles to the nearest alternative school, much of that journey along poorly lit country lanes.

You believe that schools have a vital role to play in community development, and that the proposed closure of Parkside Road High School could seriously undermine the work being done by other organisations who specifically seek to improve the sense of community in this deprived area.

Parkside Road High School

Mr and Mrs Anderson – ex-pupils

You both attended Parkside Road High School and moved into a house in the area after you married and now have two children in the school. Your own memories were not particularly happy and you don't consider yourselves to have been particularly successful at school.

When you had to choose a secondary school for your eldest child, you felt that it was very important that she should attend a school in the local area. You were delighted, however, to find that the climate of learning at Parkside Road High School was so different from what you remembered. What impressed you most was the way in which the school tried to help all pupils maximise their abilities. When you were at school, because you were not examination material, school was boring and irrelevant. Now it is exciting and your daughter and son really enjoy it.

If Parkside Road High School should close, you know that there is no school in the area that can offer the same experiences and opportunities. Any money required to improve the buildings at Parkside Road High School will be well spent.

Parkside Road High School

Transcript of interview conducted by 4th year pupils for **Radio Parkside**

Two pupils, Jane Summerfield and Kamal Mohammed interview two parents and former pupils about the threatened closure of the school.

Jane: What was it like when you came to Parkside?

Mr Anderson: Well, to be honest, I didn't really enjoy it. You see, in my day, it was a different school. The teachers didn't seem to care about you unless you were really bright or good at sport or something like that. The only good thing about it was it was where I met Angela.

Mrs Anderson: Yeh, I agree with Jim. Only the best got any encouragement and the rest of us were just child-minded. Nothing was expected of us and hardly any people stayed on to do examinations.

Kamal: Why did you send your children here then if it were that bad?

Mrs Anderson: Well things have changed a lot and anyway, it's near where we live and its much better that the children don't have to take a long bus-ride.

Mr Anderson: And also the teachers are so different nowadays. They're prepared to spend time with everybody and we know that both our children are really happy here.

Jane: What do you think about the closure then?

Mr Anderson: It's terrible. Don't you think so?

Kamal: I think it's a brilliant school.

Mrs Anderson: That's exactly what our children think. If it closes down, I don't know what we'll do. I think the council ought to spend the money on the repairs and let the teachers get on with the job. It will be awful for all of us if the school shuts down.

Kamal: Well thank you very much for talking to us. This is Kamal Mohammed...

© Mike Davis and Tim Long 1989. Basil Blackwell Ltd.

Parkside Road High School

Written assignments

1 Write a series of letters to your local newspaper in which you recreate the different points of view developed in the role-play.

2 How would you react if you heard that your school was due to close? What problems would it present to you and your school-friends? What would you look for in another school? Write a report and develop it in a playscript.

3 Describe the school experiences of Mr and Mrs Anderson. Then compare this with what their children experience. In what ways have school and schooling changed for the Anderson children?

4 Considering the advances in computer technology, imagine the education that your grand children might receive. Describe a typical day.

5 *There is more to a school's success than examination results.* Discuss.

Michelle Tyson

Teacher's notes

Michelle Tyson was based on a real story that received considerable media attention in early 1987. Since then there has been a series of cases in which the rights of mentally handicapped people have been threatened and these may be introduced to provide a context for the case of Michelle Tyson.

It may be that teachers would be wary about a role-play dealing with the sensitive issues raised here. However, in our experience, concern that pupils would react without sensitivity to the plight of the mentally handicapped has been unfounded. Similarly, we have not experienced any embarrassment relating to the central issue arising from the girl's possible future sexual behaviour.

Disturbingly, however, there was some evidence that pupils, particularly boys, were somewhat uninformed about the methods of contraception that were available. Consultation with colleagues responsible for this area of the curriculum may be of benefit. For this reason, a facsimile of the Health Education Council pamphlet *There are 8 methods of birth control* ... is reproduced on pages 98–99. Eileen Burton, in charge of Pupil Development at Queen's Park High School, believes that while young people receive contraceptive information and advice, they do not necessarily relate it to themselves until it is particularly relevant to them personally. *Michelle Tyson* helps to make the issue more relevant and reinforces what they have already been told. In Social Education terms therefore, the focus can switch from attention to Michelle Tyson as a person, to contraception as an issue. The role-play provides a context through which further explorations of the personal and social implications can be explored as an alternative to the simple provision of facts and information. The difference between Michelle Tyson and others who may experience the role-play is that Michelle is having decisions made for her, most people have to make decisions for themselves. The ability to explore decisions and the process of making them is one of the identifiable consequences of this approach.

The other feature, also mentioned in *3: Some Outcomes*, was the optimistic view that some cure for mental handicap may emerge in the future. Our discussions with people working in this field lead us to draw a number of conclusions:

- whereas a cure is extremely unlikely people with mental handicap can benefit from education and training programmes that fit them for life in the community;
- subject to the physical and mental safety and to the protection of the integrity of mentally handicapped people, there is no reason why they cannot have the range of experiences enjoyed by the rest of the population.

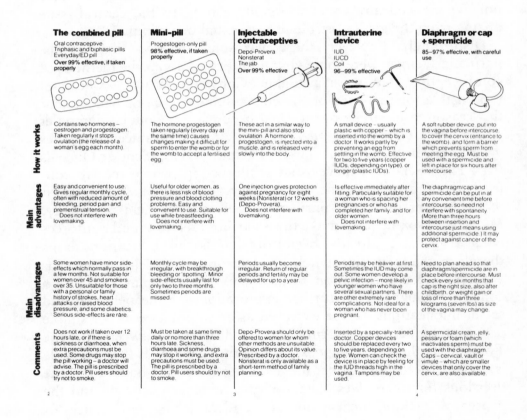

	The combined pill	**Mini-pill**	**Injectable contraceptives**	**Intrauterine device**	**Diaphragm or cap + spermicide**
	Oral contraceptive Triphasic and biphasic pills Everyday/ED pill **Over 99% effective, if taken properly**	Progestogen-only pill **98% effective, if taken properly**	Depo-Provera Noristerat The jab **Over 99% effective**	IUD IUCD Coil **96–99% effective**	**85–97% effective, with careful use**
How it works	Contains two hormones – oestrogen and progestogen. Taken regularly it stops ovulation (the release of a woman's egg each month).	The hormone progestogen taken regularly (every day at the same time) causes changes making it difficult for sperm to enter the womb or for the womb to accept a fertilised egg.	These act in a similar way to the mini-pill and also stop ovulation. A hormone progestogen, is injected into a muscle, and is released very slowly into the body.	A small device – usually plastic with copper – which is inserted into the womb by a doctor. It works partly by preventing an egg from settling in the womb. Effective for two to five years (copper IUDs, depending on type), or longer (plastic IUDs).	A soft rubber device, put into the vagina before intercourse, to cover the cervix (entrance to the womb), and form a barrier which prevents sperm from meeting the egg. Must be used with a spermicide and left in place for six hours after intercourse.
Main advantages	Easy and convenient to use. Gives regular monthly cycle, often with reduced amount of bleeding, period pain and premenstrual tension. Does not interfere with lovemaking.	Useful for older women, as there is less risk of blood pressure and blood clotting problems. Easy and convenient to use. Suitable for use while breastfeeding. Does not interfere with lovemaking.	One injection gives protection against pregnancy for eight weeks (Noristerat) or 12 weeks (Depo-Provera). Does not interfere with lovemaking.	Is effective immediately after fitting. Particularly suitable for a woman who is spacing her pregnancies or who has completed her family, and for older women. Does not interfere with lovemaking.	The diaphragm/cap and spermicide can be put in at any convenient time before intercourse, so need not interfere with spontaneity. (More than three hours between insertion and intercourse just means using additional spermicide.) It may protect against cancer of the cervix.
Main disadvantages	Some women have minor side-effects which normally pass in a few months. Not suitable for women over 45 and smokers over 35. Unsuitable for those with a personal or family history of strokes, heart attacks or raised blood pressure, and some diabetics. Serious side-effects are rare.	Monthly cycle may be irregular, with breakthrough bleeding or 'spotting'. Minor side-effects usually last for only two to three months. Sometimes periods are missed.	Periods usually become irregular. Return of regular periods and fertility may be delayed for up to a year.	Periods may be heavier at first. Sometimes the IUD may come out. Some women develop a pelvic infection – more likely in younger women who have several sexual partners. There are other extremely rare complications. Not ideal for a woman who has never been pregnant.	Need to plan ahead so that diaphragm/spermicide are in place before intercourse. Must check every six months that cap is the right size, also after childbirth, or weight gain or loss of more than three kilograms (seven lbs) as size of the vagina may change.
Comments	Does not work if taken over 12 hours late, or if there is sickness or diarrhoea, when extra precautions must be used. Some drugs may stop the pill working – a doctor will advise. The pill is prescribed by a doctor. Pill users should try not to smoke.	Must be taken at same time daily or no more than three hours late. Sickness, diarrhoea and some drugs may stop it working, and extra precautions must be used. The pill is prescribed by a doctor. Pill users should try not to smoke.	Depo-Provera should only be offered to women for whom other methods are unsuitable. Opinion differs about its value. Prescribed by a doctor. Noristerat is only available as a short-term method of family planning.	Inserted by a specially-trained doctor. Copper devices should be replaced every two to five years, depending on type. Women can check the device is in place by feeling for the IUD threads high in the vagina. Tampons may be used.	A spermicidal cream, jelly, pessary or foam (which inactivates sperm) must be used with the diaphragm. Caps – cervical, vault or vimule – which are smaller devices that only cover the cervix, are also available.

2   3   4

Whether these views would get in the way of a successful playing of Michelle Tyson, we are not sure. It would be for individual teachers to judge whether these issues were explored in advance of, or after the role-play, or not at all. We can only repeat that young people showed remarkable sensitivity to the issues and to the plight of Michelle and her family.

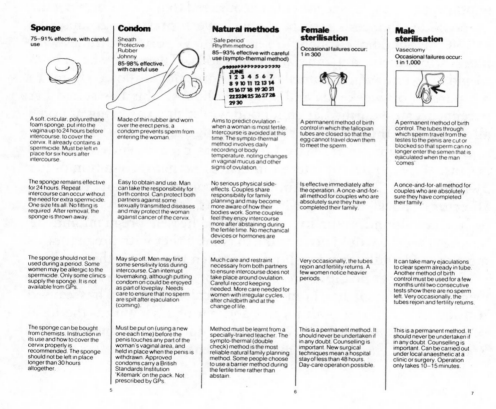

Sponge	**Condom**	**Natural methods**	**Female sterilisation**	**Male sterilisation**
75–91% effective, with careful use	Sheath Protective Rubber Johnny 85-98% effective, with careful use	'Safe period' Rhythm method 85–93% effective with careful use (sympto-thermal method)	Occasional failures occur: 1 in 300	Vasectomy Occasional failures occur: 1 in 1,000
A soft, circular, polyurethane foam sponge, put into the vagina up to 24 hours before intercourse, to cover the cervix. It already contains a spermicide. Must be left in place for six hours after intercourse.	Made of thin rubber and worn over the erect penis, a condom prevents sperm from entering the woman.	Aims to predict ovulation – when a woman is most fertile. Intercourse is avoided at this time. The sympto-thermal method involves daily recording of body temperature, noting changes in vaginal mucus and other signs of ovulation.	A permanent method of birth control in which the fallopian tubes are closed so that the egg cannot travel down them to meet the sperm.	A permanent method of birth control. The tubes through which sperm travel from the testes to the penis are cut or blocked so that sperm can no longer enter the semen that is ejaculated when the man 'comes'.
The sponge remains effective for 24 hours. Repeat intercourse can occur without the need for extra spermicide. One size fits all. No fitting is required. After removal, the sponge is thrown away.	Easy to obtain and use. Man can take the responsibility for birth control. Can protect both partners against some sexually transmitted diseases and may protect the woman against cancer of the cervix.	No serious physical side-effects. Couples share responsibility for family planning and may become more aware of how their bodies work. Some couples feel they enjoy intercourse more after abstaining during the fertile time. No mechanical devices or hormones are used.	Is effective immediately after the operation. A once-and-for-all method for couples who are absolutely sure they have completed their family.	A once-and-for-all method for couples who are absolutely sure they have completed their family.
The sponge should not be used during a period. Some women may be allergic to the spermicide. Only some clinics supply the sponge. It is not available from GPs.	May slip off. Men may find some sensitivity loss during intercourse. Can interrupt lovemaking, although putting condom on could be enjoyed as part of loveplay. Needs care to ensure that no sperm are spilt after ejaculation (coming).	Much care and restraint necessary from both partners to ensure intercourse does not take place around ovulation. Careful record keeping needed. More care needed for women with irregular cycles, after childbirth and at the change of life.	Very occasionally, the tubes rejoin and fertility returns. A few women notice heavier periods.	It can take many ejaculations to clear sperm already in tube. Another method of birth control must be used for a few months until two consecutive tests show there are no sperm left. Very occasionally, the tubes rejoin and fertility returns.
The sponge can be bought from chemists. Instruction in its use and how to cover the cervix properly is recommended. The sponge should not be left in place longer than 30 hours altogether.	Must be put on (using a new one each time) before the penis touches any part of the woman's vaginal area, and held in place when the penis is withdrawn. Approved condoms carry a British Standards Institution 'Kitemark' on the pack. Not prescribed by GPs.	Method must be learnt from a specially-trained teacher. The sympto-thermal (double check) method is the most reliable natural family planning method. Some people choose to use a barrier method during the fertile time rather than abstain.	This is a permanent method. It should never be undertaken if in any doubt. Counselling is important. New surgical techniques mean a hospital stay of less than 48 hours. Day-care operation possible.	This is a permanent method. It should never be undertaken if in any doubt. Counselling is important. Can be carried out under local anaesthetic at a clinic or surgery. Operation only takes 10–15 minutes.
5		6		7

Michelle Tyson

Background information

Michelle Tyson is a seventeen year, eleven month old girl who has been in the care of the Local Authority since she was six and according to some medical evidence, supported by the Director of the home she lives in, she has a mental age of five. She is in need of constant care and supervision although she is capable of doing some things for herself, like dressing and feeding. She has a limited vocabulary and has difficulty expressing herself.

A few years ago she would have spent all of her life in a closed institution but because of changing attitudes towards mentally handicapped people, she is being encouraged to lead as normal a life as possible. Pioneering such changes were pressure groups like MENCAP, who have sought to replace the Victorian attitudes with more sympathetic and humane conditions. Therefore she spends Monday to Friday in a council nursing home but is allowed home to her parents on weekends and school holidays. This has suited her parents because during her childhood whilst she was living at home all of the time they found her an increasingly unbearable strain.

Concern amongst her Care Officers has been recently expressed because of her apparent interest in males and her recognition of her own sexuality. The Local Authority is concerned about this. The Director of Social Services, Mr Peter Scott, fears that in responding to her new-found sexuality, she will get herself pregnant and he believes that she would not be able to cope, either with pregnancy or motherhood and that steps should be taken to prevent this arising.

News of the possible sterilisation of Michelle, leaked by a member of staff of her home to the local newspaper has caused considerable concern both locally and nationally. Within the local community, Fr Frank McGee has taken up the issue and the Civil Rights Movement have also made representations.

Michelle Tyson

Background information, *continued*

You are a committee who have been called together to give advice to the Local Authority and you will have the chance to discover the views of all of the interested parties before making a recommendation as to what should happen to Michelle.

The options you have to consider include one or more of the following:

1 Sterilisation of Michelle to ensure no possibility of pregnancy;
2 The supervised use of some form of contraceptive, mechanical or chemical;
3 The placing of Michelle in a single-sex secure environment;
4 Returning her to the care and control of her parents;
5 Leaving her in the home and expecting the staff to supervise her and others' behaviour.

Michelle Tyson

Director of council home – Miss Charlotte Smith

You have overall responsibility for twenty young handicapped children of both sexes, ranging from eleven to twenty-five years old. Each child demands a considerable amount of attention which you find difficult to provide, owing to a lack of staff resources. You believe that Michelle's increasing sexual awareness could lead to an unwanted pregnancy which you feel the home would be unable to support. In the past teenage girls have been given contraceptive pills but these would be inappropriate in Michelle's case as she receives other medication for the treatment of her epilepsy. Although you are aware of the moral considerations of the case, your prime concern and responsibility is for the maximising of resources and the efficient running of the home. In an ideal situation she would not need to be sterilised, since she would be under constant supervision. However this is not practicable given the resources available to you.

Michelle Tyson

Parish Priest – Fr Frank McGee

You are the Catholic Priest in the parish where Mr and Mrs Tyson live. You have known the family for fifteen years and have watched as Mr and Mrs Tyson have struggled to cope with bringing up Michelle. Whilst you understand the feelings of the professionals in the home and the parents, your concerns are of a religious nature. For you, the capacity to give birth is a God-given right which should not under *any* circumstances be denied.

Michelle Tyson

Letter to a national newspaper

Dear Sir

I read with alarm the proposal that Michelle Tyson, a mentally handicapped seventeen year old, is to be sterilised on the recommendation of the Council's Social Services Department.

I believe that a decision to sterilise Michelle would be completely retrograde. This girl is in danger of being treated like an animal and, not to put too fine a point on it, she is to be spayed like an animal. In my opinion, this is going back to the days when a mentally handicapped person was considered not to be human. I think that some other form of care and contraception should be considered.

If this barbaric step is taken, I fear that other cases will be queueing up in the wings and sterilisation will become the norm for mentally handicapped people.

We cannot stand by and allow such a thing to happen.

Foster

Dr Sara Foster
Action for Mentally Handicapped

Michelle Tyson

Mr and Mrs Tyson

You never recovered from the shock of the realisation that your second child Michelle, born one year after her sister, was mentally handicapped. Although you struggled for her first six years you found it an intolerable strain which nearly broke up your marriage. Although you love Michelle as much as her sister who is a normal child, you would never wish for the birth of another handicapped child and you feel sure that Michelle could never give birth to a normal baby. What is more, were she to have a baby, normal or not, you can see no way that she would be able to cope with either pregnancy or childrearing.

Michelle Tyson

Press release from Director of Social Services – Mr Peter Scott

Though it grieves me to do so, I feel that it is my duty to decide who can and who cannot cope in normal society. In Michelle's case I do not consider that she will ever be able to control her own sexuality and that she would be open to abuse from unscrupulous or unknowing members of society. What is more, Michelle could never relate pregnancy to sexual activity, nor could she derive any benefit or enjoyment from motherhood. In the event of her giving birth the child would almost certainly become an additional burden on my department. The only other alternative, which I do not consider acceptable, would be for Michelle to undergo a series of abortions throughout her child-bearing years.

Michelle Tyson

Civil Rights Movement Representative – Ms Farida Patel

For you, the suggestion to sterilise this girl is Nazi almost. It constitutes a highly dangerous precedent where many members of society may find themselves as targets for this sort of treatment. You fear that this could even be a step towards the introduction of sterilisation for social control purposes, that women could be sterilised for a variety of intellectual, emotional and economic reasons. To treat somebody who is very close to being an adult, differently from an adult, worries you indeed. Were she one month older, nobody would be able to suggest sterilisation as a possible option. Furthermore, you strongly object to the finality of such an act from which there will be no point of return even should there be advances made in the treatment of handicapped children and adults.

Michelle Tyson

Written assignments

1 A conference is to take place to discuss the case of Michelle Tyson. Those present will be:

Miss Charlotte Smith, Director of the Council Home;
Father Frank McGee, Parish Priest;
Dr Sara Foster, Action for Mentally Handicapped representative;
Ms Farida Patel, representative of Civil Rights Movement

Imagine the conference. Present the views of each person there. If you like you can set out your assignment like a play, but remember to indicate the feelings of the speakers.

2 Mr and Mrs Tyson have been asked to take part in a TV programme about the problems of bringing up a mentally handicapped child. Think carefully about the sort of questions they might be asked and about how each one would respond. Remember that Mr and Mrs Tyson will have experienced the problems differently. Write the interview.

3 Write an essay which clearly describes all of the issues that are involved in the case of Michelle Tyson. Next sum up all of the possible solutions. If the decision was yours, how would you treat Michelle? Remember you have to try to find a solution that is best for everyone. You may have to disregard the views of one or more of those involved. Whose views would you disregard? Why? Describe how you came to your decision regarding the case of Michelle Tyson and why you think that yours is the best course of action.

Cheryl Wilson

Teacher's notes

Cheryl Wilson is one of the thousands of school girls who become pregnant every year. The authors deliberately chose to include this highly sensitive issue for certain reasons, some of which were identified by a head of Year at a trial school. She felt that the role-play was successful because:

- it didn't demand high levels of literacy;
- there was no need for acting ability;
- more conventional methods of tackling the issue (open discussion, debate) could be extremely difficult for young people to handle;
- participants became involved and committed without having to 'own' the opinions or ideas they were expressing;
- it did not impose an orthodoxy – it was deliberately 'doubtful' and value free.

The experience of trialling it was remarkable for the extent to which support was expressed for Cheryl having the baby despite her own expressed wishes. Recommendations beyond that included, her parents bringing up the child, it being placed for adoption, her leaving school to raise it, marrying John and going to night school to continue her study. Anti-abortion groups would have been delighted at the positions adopted by the young people.

Cheryl Wilson

Background information

Cheryl Wilson is a fifteen year, ten month old girl who lives with her parents and elder sisters. She attends a local comprehensive school where she is expected to do very well in GCSE examinations. Her early ambition was to go to medical school.

She has been going out with John Astley since the beginning of the fourth year and it was a shock to her to discover during the first term of the fifth year that she had become pregnant.

There are a number of courses of action open to her and you will now have an opportunity to talk to some of the people closely involved in her predicament. These will be:

> Cheryl herself
> John Astley – Boyfriend
> Mr Jack Wilson – Father
> Mrs Michaela Wilson – Mother
> Mrs Karen Burton – Childcare Teacher/Form Tutor
> Dr Sebastian Cooper – Family Doctor.

When you have spoken to them all, you will be required to recommend an appropriate response to Cheryl's predicament.

Cheryl Wilson

Cheryl Wilson

You were aware of the risks you were taking by sleeping with John but you never thought that you would become pregnant. You had tried to get contraceptives from your doctor but he had been unsympathetic saying that he would have to notify your parents if you insisted on having the pill prescribed, something you didn't want to happen.

Despite not having any contraceptives, you continued having sexual relations with John, hoping that 'it wouldn't happen to you'. You now bitterly regret this and wish that you had listened to the advice given to you at school in Childcare classes.

You want to have an abortion. You cannot face the prospect of being a mother at your age, you would have to leave school, become entirely dependent on your parents, give up any prospects of higher education and miss all the fun of being a teenager. You know girls who have become mothers because the idea seemed good at the time. You now see them as little more than drudges, tied to domestic chores with no life of their own.

What is more, you think it unfair on the child to be brought up in those circumstances.

You are eight weeks pregnant and you want to have the abortion as soon as possible. Although your parents have been very supportive you know that they want you to have the baby. You have been told that until you are sixteen you require parental permission for the abortion. Your parents have refused to have anything to do with it and your only alternative is to wait until your sixteenth birthday. There is one major problem, this will bring you to within days of the safe limit for abortions to be carried out. You do not want to wait this long, you need your parents' permission as soon as possible. You also need financial help as the abortion will cost £200 if you cannot get one on the National Health Service.

Cheryl Wilson

John Astley – Boyfriend

You don't know what to do. You feel really guilty about putting Cheryl in this position and you are particularly worried about the possible consequences. You know that if she was to have the baby she would have to leave school and miss her chance of doing 'A' levels and going to university.

You have thought about asking her to marry you but realise that you could not keep her without giving up your own ambitions to get a job as an apprentice car mechanic. Your parents have refused to discuss the matter with you and have not given you any support at all. You are also very worried that you might be prosecuted by the police because Cheryl is below the age of consent.

The idea of being a father at the age of sixteen also appals you and although you are very fond of Cheryl you can't imagine settling down with her, or anyone else come to that. You just wish that the problem would go away. You have talked to Cheryl about the possibilities and she has made it quite clear to you that she is going to decide what she is going to do.

Cheryl Wilson

Mr Jack Wilson – Father

When you first heard that Cheryl was pregnant you wanted to give John a real hiding. You were outraged that he took advantage of her without having to live with the consequences. Cheryl was doing so well at school and her teacher said that she was university material. Now, all of that is out of the question because she will have to leave school to bring up her child.

The idea of John doing the honourable thing, if indeed it has occurred to him, is not acceptable to you at all. However, you and your wife intend to do everything possible to support your daughter and will do your best to help her become a good mother to the child.

You know that this whole thing has brought shame on your family but there is no point crying over spilt milk. Cheryl is simply going to have to face up to the fact that she is to become a mother.

Cheryl has expressed to you a wish to have an abortion but she needs your permission, something which you will not grant. Even if she could arrange the abortion herself, you could not support it. She doesn't understand that you cannot treat human life so casually. Whether she likes it or not she has to face up to her responsibilities and accept her new role as a mother.

Cheryl Wilson

Mrs Michaela Wilson – Mother

Although you are disappointed that Cheryl did not wait to get married before she got pregnant you don't think that it's the end of the world. You know that Cheryl is upset that she is going to be unable to finish her studies but she will soon get over this when she realises the pleasures of motherhood.

You always found it strange that Cheryl was so keen to go to medical school, not something that you thought was a good idea. It seemed odd to you that she intended spending so much time studying when she would probably get married and have children anyway and not have to work.

You think that the only reason Cheryl wants an abortion is that she is frightened of giving birth and you remember feeling the same when you had your first baby when you were eighteen. You also realise that she might be worried about being a single parent but you and your husband intend to support her all you can until she finds a nice boy to marry.

You never expected to be a grandma so young but you quite look forward to it now that you have got used to the idea.

Cheryl Wilson

Mrs Karen Burton – Childcare Teacher/Form Tutor

You have been painstaking in trying to educate pupils so that they avoid falling into this very trap. Cheryl has been attending your Childcare lessons since the beginning of the fourth year and as an intelligent girl you are amazed that she should have allowed such a situation to occur. Whilst not involving yourself in the private lives of your pupils you have made it clear to them that if they choose to be sexually active they have a responsibility to themselves to take proper precautions. All of your pupils knew where to go if they needed contraceptives even in the event of family doctors not being willing to prescribe them.

When Cheryl came to you seeking advice you were aware of a number of conflicting responses. You were greatly disappointed that Cheryl had failed to take the appropriate measures which she was aware of, you were annoyed at the attitude of the family doctor in refusing to prescribe suitable contraceptives, you were also annoyed at Cheryl for not going to an alternative family planning clinic.

You pointed out to her two crucial factors:

1 being under sixteen, she needs parental consent for an abortion. If this is refused, her only alternative is to apply to become a ward of court;

2 Though she will be sixteen in two months time and be able at that time to sign her own consent form, she will be perilously close to the safe limit for abortions. She will only have a few days in which to have the operation. Moreover, the longer she delays the more complex the operation and the greater risk to her health.

Cheryl seems set upon having the abortion even though you know that she lacks any parental support for that course of action. You do, however, believe that she has thought seriously about it and that her decision is a reasoned one. You have offered to talk to her parents but you know that this is really a family matter and you do not have high hopes of convincing them of Cheryl's right to make up her own mind.

Cheryl Wilson

Dr Sebastian Cooper – Family Doctor

When Cheryl Wilson came to your surgery asking to be prescribed the contraceptive pill, you said the same to her as you would to any girl under the age of consent, that you would only prescribe it after consulting with the parents.

Whilst you are aware of statistics which suggest that in the absence of any contraception the number of unwanted pregnancies amongst teenage girls increases, you still believe absolute caution is required before administering contraceptive pills. What is more, you are not sure that prescribing contraceptive pills is in the best long-term health interests of the person involved.

Privately, you do not agree with easy access to contraceptives which in your opinion only serves to encourage sexual promiscuity, particularly amongst the young.

When Cheryl's parents brought her to your surgery for the pregnancy test, you found it hard to hide your annoyance at her carelessness and reckless behaviour. Fortunately for her, both parents are standing by her and you are pleased to see that they do not favour abortion, something that you believe is all too easy to obtain in today's society. In your view, the only circumstances in which abortion can be considered are:

a) if the health of the prospective mother is at risk; and/or

b) if the child is likely to be born suffering from physical or mental handicap.

It is unlikely that in Cheryl's case, either of these will apply.

Cheryl Wilson

Written assignments

1 Write the conversation between Cheryl and Karen Burton when Cheryl first tells Karen Burton about her being pregnant.

2 Describe in any written form you choose the reactions of a) John Astley, b) Jack Wilson and c) Michaela Wilson when they first hear the news that Cheryl is pregnant.

3 Mrs Wilson believes that Cheryl doesn't need education and qualifications because she will probably get married and have children. Do you agree or disagree with Mrs Wilson about women's role in society? Write a letter of about 250 words to a newspaper either agreeing or disagreeing with Mrs Wilson. Then write a reply to your letter of about the same length.

4 Cheryl was aware of the risks she was taking but ignored them. Write and design a leaflet, a poster or an information pack that Cheryl might have taken further notice of.

George York

Teacher's notes

If the popular press is to be believed, the majority of the population, including young people, support the return of capital punishment in cases of murder. The most remarkable outcome of *George York* therefore is the support given by most groups to parole. This does not mean that the debate is any less intense, rather that the balance comes down in favour of George being allowed to return to society and *make up for (his) dreadful crime in whatever little ways (he) can* as he says in his written submission to the Parole Board.

This unexpected outcome can form the basis of much further work, both written and oral. The subject of capital punishment seems to come up at least once a year in the House of Commons and when it does there is a great deal of comment in the media for young people to consider. Letters, articles and even formal debates could stem quite naturally from the public discussion.

George York

Report to Parole Board

Prisoner's name: George York.
Number: 79/64137GY
Sex: Male
Date of Birth: 4th October 1953
Offence: Murder
Sentence: Life Imprisonment

Trial Synopsis: York pleaded not guilty to murder but guilty to manslaughter of his wife, Jeanette, during a violent domestic dispute. Convicted by majority verdict.

Prisons: 4 years Strangeways, 5 years Castle Milne

In accordance with established procedure, this prisoner is now eligible to be reviewed by this Parole Board.

You will have the opportunity to discover the views of the following people:

> Colonel Frank Lamb – Prison Governor
> Mrs Hilda Wheeler – Senior Probation Officer
> Mrs Sheila Anderton – Jeanette York's mother
> Mr Paul York – George's brother
> Dr Robert Hughes – Prison Doctor
> Mrs Margaret Campbell MP – Pro-Hanging Campaigner

You will also receive a written submission from George York, himself.

When you have considered all of the points of view, you will be asked to recommend parole or the continuation of the sentence.

George York

Further notes

Parole

Parole is a way of giving prisoners the opportunity to leave prison before their sentences have expired.

Prisoners are usually eligible after they have served a third of their sentence.

While on parole they are under the supervision of a Probation Officer until their sentence has run its full course. In the case of 'lifers' this is for the rest of their lives.

In the event of a parolee re-offending, s/he can be recalled to prison. A lifer on parole can be recalled to prison if the Probation Officer believes that s/he may re-offend.

George York

Report from Colonel Frank Lamb – Prison Governor

My contact with York during the last five years has been limited but this is because he has presented my staff with no problems. He is, in many ways, an ideal prisoner. In my opinion his progress has exemplified one of the things that prisons are supposed to do, that is, to rehabilitate criminals and prepare them for return to society.

I do not condone his crime, which was indeed a particularly violent one but I recognise that he has shown genuine remorse and that he actively sought to make amends by his behaviour towards other prisoners and prison staff. He has befriended prisoners many of whom are inadequate socially and educationally, has written letters for them and has set an example of how to accept the prison sentence.

He has come to terms with why he is in prison and recognises the justice of the sentence. My concern now is that he, as still a relatively young man, should be allowed to return to society and be allowed to lead as normal a life as possible under the circumstances. I also firmly believe that it is important that he is released now, lest his indeterminate prison sentence undoes the progress that he has made so far.

I firmly recommend him for parole.

George York

Mrs Hilda Wheeler – Senior Probation Officer

You have interviewed York on a number of occasions during the last twelve months and after consultation with colleagues, have reached the conclusion that he should be recommended for parole for the following reasons:

   a) you no longer think that he is a threat to society, there is little likelihood of a repeat offence;

   b) the original offence took place within domestic circumstances which clearly no longer prevail;

   c) his brother, Paul York, has offered him suitable accommodation away from the area where the crime took place.

You feel it necessary to make it clear what responsibilities and authority the Probation Service would have if he were to be released on licence:

   a) since murder requires a mandatory life sentence, he can be recalled at any time on the recommendation of his supervising officer;

   b) if, at any time, his behaviour gives cause for concern, he can be recalled immediately to continue his sentence;

   c) the supervising officer can demand attendance at the Probation Office at any time and failure to co-operate will result in immediate withdrawal of parole.

Given the extent of the supervision available and the powers of recall to prison, plus his obvious improvement, you feel confident that parole would be a suitable next step in the rehabilitation of George York.

George York

Mrs Sheila Anderton – Jeanette York's mother

York killed your daughter and he should have been hanged. He made her life a constant misery, he beat her, kept her short of money and worst of all, always unjustly blamed her for the loss of their baby. A man who stabs his wife to death can be nothing short of evil.

You have heard that his case is being considered for parole. As far as you are concerned, he has no case to be released. He murdered a young girl and if he was let out, he would do it again because that's the sort of man he is.

If we cannot hang murderers, the least we can do is keep them behind bars for the rest of their lives. Why should killers be allowed to live in the relative comfort of our jails when their victims are dead? York should stay where he is until his dying day, which you hope is soon.

You have written to your MP, who you know agrees with you about hanging. She has said that she is going to make representations to the authorities.

George York

Mr Paul York – George's brother

You don't for a minute pretend that George had any justification for what he did to Jeanette and it took you several years before you were willing to talk to him again. It was when he started writing to you that you realised that your refusal to see him needed rethinking.

You saw him first when he was transferred to the open prison and you realised then that he felt real remorse and that he accepted the full horror of his crime. As time went by, you saw that he was a changed man, he was caring and considerate and he clearly wanted to make amends for his crime.

When the issue of his parole came up you felt that you wanted to be part of his return to normal society and this is why you offered him a home with you and your wife. You both wanted to show your faith in his development.

You know that there are people who feel that he should spend the rest of his life in prison and, to a certain extent, you can understand the strong feelings of Jeanette's mother but what would be achieved by keeping a man in prison for the rest of his life?

You believe that he should be given the chance to pay back his debt to society by making a useful contribution to it. This is something he himself is determined to do.

George York

Dr Robert Hughes – Prison Doctor

It is part of your statutory duties to maintain regular checks on the physical and mental health of the inmates of your prison. You have therefore seen York on a regular basis over the last four years.

There was no suggestion at the time of his crime that he was suffering from any serious form of mental disorder and there has been no evidence since to suggest that he has any form of mental illness other than periodic slight depression, not uncommon amongst long-term prisoners.

Physically and mentally he has adjusted well to prison life, which you think reflects his positive understanding of the nature and intention of imprisonment. You believe that he will experience few problems in returning to the outside world, particularly within the context of a supportive family environment such as his brother has offered.

Criminal behaviour can never be described in precise medical terms. It is impossible to say for definite that a person will never offend again, just as it is impossible to predict who, in society, is likely to be a murderer. However, in your professional opinion and on the basis of your knowledge of him you feel as confident as you can be that he will not offend again if he is allowed parole.

George York

Transcript of TV programme featuring Mrs Margaret Campbell MP: Pro-Hanging Campaigner

Interviewer: What is your general view of how murderers should be treated?

Mrs Campbell: An eye for an eye, a tooth for a tooth! is my firm belief. Those who murder have no right to remain a part of the society in which they live. They have transgressed the laws of their society in such a way as to deprive them of the right to re-admittance. The only proper response that society can make is to bring back hanging.

Interviewer: Do you really believe that hanging is a deterrent?

Mrs Campbell: I have little doubt that a man, faced with the prospect of the death penalty would think twice before taking another person's life. The people of this country know that and constantly demand the return of hanging. Just think of the Yorkshire Ripper and the foul murders he committed. Surely a man like this has no right to live after the lives he has taken? No, I believe firmly that the punishment should fit the crime. Murder should be punished by death.

Interviewer: I know that you have recently been involved in the case of George York. What exactly is your attitude towards the possibility of his parole?

Mrs Campbell: The idea of a man like George York walking free, after his horrendous crime appals me and all sensible people and has caused great distress to his dead wife's mother. What is more, his release would make a mockery of the courts. The life sentence was supposed to replace the death penalty, but life sentences are not what they pretend to be. Often a murderer will only serve a fraction of his sentence and certainly won't stay behind bars for all of his life.

George York

Transcript of TV programme featuring Mrs Margaret Campbell MP: Pro-Hanging Campaigner,

continued

Interviewer: But York has been in gaol for nine years. Surely he has satisfied society's need for justice.

Mrs Campbell: York has only served nine years. His wife, were she alive, would be a young woman of thirty-three. It is an insult to her memory that his release is even being considered. I will do all in my power to oppose his parole.

Interviewer: Well thank you, Mrs Campbell. I am sure your views will provoke much interest.

George York

Statement by George York

H.M. Prison
Castle Milne, Wiltshire
Number 79/64 13784

Dear Sir

I believe that my sentence is due for review and that I am being considered for release on licence. I understand that I have the right to present my case for consideration.

I have tried very hard to behave properly since my imprisonment. I know all prisoners probably say the same but I am a changed man. I don't want to make any excuses for my crime because there aren't any. To this day, I don't know why I did it but I did kill Jeanette and I know that was wrong. I will never get over my feelings of guilt whether I am in prison or not.

My brother Paul and his wife have offered to take me into their home and being there will give me the chance to make a fresh start in life and to pay my debt to society far more usefully than being behind bars. I have been in prison now for nine years and I don't feel that I can change for the better any more. I want to get out and show people that I am changed and that I want to make up for my dreadful crime in whatever little ways I can.

I know that there are people who still hate me like Jeanette's mother and I don't blame them for their feelings. I only hope I can be given the opportunity to show them that they are wrong and that I am not as evil as some people make out.

Yours faithfully

George York.

George York

Written assignments

1 Imagine you are George York. Describe how it feels to be in prison.

2 *An eye for an eye, a tooth for a tooth!* How useful is this as a basis for a sentencing policy? Write a magazine article of about 500 words.

3 What problems do you anticipate George York facing if he is allowed parole?

4 Write the newspaper reports describing Jeanette York's murder and George's arrest and trial.

5 Describe a radio or TV interview with Colonel Frank Lamb and Mrs Margaret Campbell.

General written assignments

The following assignments can be applicable to any of the role plays.

1 Rewrite the events described in the role play as a story. You must include all of the characters that you have met and you may, if you wish, invent other characters.

2 Write an essay outlining the major issues that this case raises. You may wish to focus on the information presented by one or two individuals.

3 Write an essay describing the decision made by your group and how that decision was reached. Compare your recommendation(s) to those made by other groups and attempt to explain how and why those recommendations differed from yours.

4 For role players only. Describe the experience of taking on a role. You may wish to consider some of the following: How easy was it to become the character? How easy was it to cope with the questions you were asked? How did you react to the decisions made? What would your decision be?